Mythology, Myths, and Legends
MYTHOLOGY
OF THE
EGYPTIANS
Don Nardo
Enslow Publishers, Inc.
40 Industrial Road
Box 398
Berkeley Heights, NJ 07922
USA
http://www.enslow.com

Originally published as *Egyptian Mythology* in 2001.



**Library of Congress Cataloging-in-Publication Data**

Nardo, Don, 1947– author.
Mythology of the Egyptians / Don Nardo. — [New edition.]
pages cm. — (Mythology, myths, and legends)
Originally published under the title Egyptian mythology. Berkeley Heights,
J : Enslow Publishers, 2001.
Audience: Grades 7 to 8.
Includes bibliographical references and index.
ISBN 978-0-7660-6167-5
1. Mythology, Egyptian—Juvenile literature. 2. Gods, Egyptian—Juvenile
Literature. I. Title.
BL2441.3.N38 2014
398.20962—dc23
2014007410

**Future Editions:**
Paperback ISBN: 978-0-7660-6168-2
EPUB ISBN: 978-0-7660-6169-9
Single-User PDF ISBN: 978-0-7660-6170-5
Multi-User PDF ISBN: 978-0-7660-6171-2

Printed in the United States of America
072014 HF Group, North Manchester, IN
10 9 8 7 6 5 4 3 2 1

**To Our Readers:** We have done our best to make sure all Internet addresses in this book were active and appropriate when we went to press. However, the author and the publisher have no control over and assume no liability for the material available on those Internet sites or on other Web sites they may link to. Comments can be sent by e-mail to comments@enslow.com or to the address on the back cover.

Cover and Illustrations by William Sauts Bock

# Contents

# PREFACE

The nature of the gods in Egyptian mythology, along with their deeds and the customs surrounding their worship, strongly reflected the physical characteristics of the country and its unique culture. Other characters in Egypt's myths also reflect the local heritage.

Egypt is a land of marked physical extremes. Situated in the northeastern sector of Africa, the country consists primarily of dry desert wastelands stretching for hundreds of miles in all directions. Almost all of the ancient Egyptians lived in a narrow, very fertile strip of land bordering the Nile River. From the highlands of Ethiopia in the south, the Nile flows to the Mediterranean Sea in the north. It was in this pleasant and productive Nile valley, irrigated by the river, that the ancient Egyptians built the world's first great civilization.

## Thirty Centuries of Dynasties and Pharaohs

The beginnings of that civilization, which lasted for many thousands of years, are lost in the mists of time. But historians know that as early as 4500 B.C. (about 6,500 years ago), Egypt consisted of two separate regions, each with a relatively advanced culture in which people lived together in villages, farmed the land, and raised livestock. Slowly, these two separate regions grew into kingdoms ruled by monarchs. One of the kingdoms, Upper Egypt, stretched from Aswan, in the far south, northward to the city of Memphis. The other, Lower Egypt, was composed of the lands north of Memphis, including the fan-shaped, very fertile Nile delta, where the river empties into the Mediterranean Sea. (The Egyptians based their conception of Upper and Lower regions on the direction in which the Nile flows. To them, the river's source seemed "up," or north, and its end pointed "down," or south, whereas on a modern map the Nile flows from south to north.)

These two kingdoms finally became united into one country sometime between 3150 and 3100 B.C. by Menes, a powerful king of Upper Egypt. He took the title of pharaoh and established his capital at Memphis. Thereafter, all of Egypt's rulers were called pharaohs. Menes also founded the first dynasty (a succession of rulers, all of whom belonged to the same family) in Egypt.[1]

In the two thousand years following Menes's unification of Egypt, the country attained its greatest level of power, influence, and cultural achievement. For convenience, modern historians divide this long period into several shorter ones. The period encompassing the First and Second Dynasties, in which sixteen pharaohs reigned, is referred to both as the Early Dynastic Period and the Archaic Period (around 3100–2690 B.C.). Next came the period called the Old Kingdom (around 2690–2180 B.C.), in which most of the great pyramids were erected; then a short intermediate period; then the Middle Kingdom (around 2055–1650 B.C.), in which trade with other peoples greatly expanded and Egypt absorbed much of Nubia, a region lying to its south; then another short intermediate period; and finally the New Kingdom (around 1550–1070 B.C.), in which a series of powerful pharaohs conquered other parts of the Near East, creating a great Egyptian empire.[2]

Following the end of the New Kingdom, Egypt entered a long period of decline under mostly weak rulers, followed by Persians, Greeks, and other foreigners who had seized the throne. Eventually, in 31 B.C., the Romans, who had by then built a huge and powerful Mediterranean empire, defeated Egypt's last independent ruler—the famous Cleopatra VII (who was actually Greek). In the thirty centuries from Menes to Cleopatra, more than two hundred pharaohs, belonging to some thirty dynasties, had ruled the country.

# THE GODS

Ogdoad gods
as Man
Amun
as Honker Goose
Nu
Naunet
Hey
Hauhet
Kek
Kauket
Amaunet
Mediterranean
LOWER EGYPT
Heliopolis
GIZA
MEMPHIS
EGYPT
Hermopolis
Nile River
UPPER EGYPT
GREAT SPHINX and PYRAMIDS at GIZA
Aswan
Thebes

# OF EGYPT

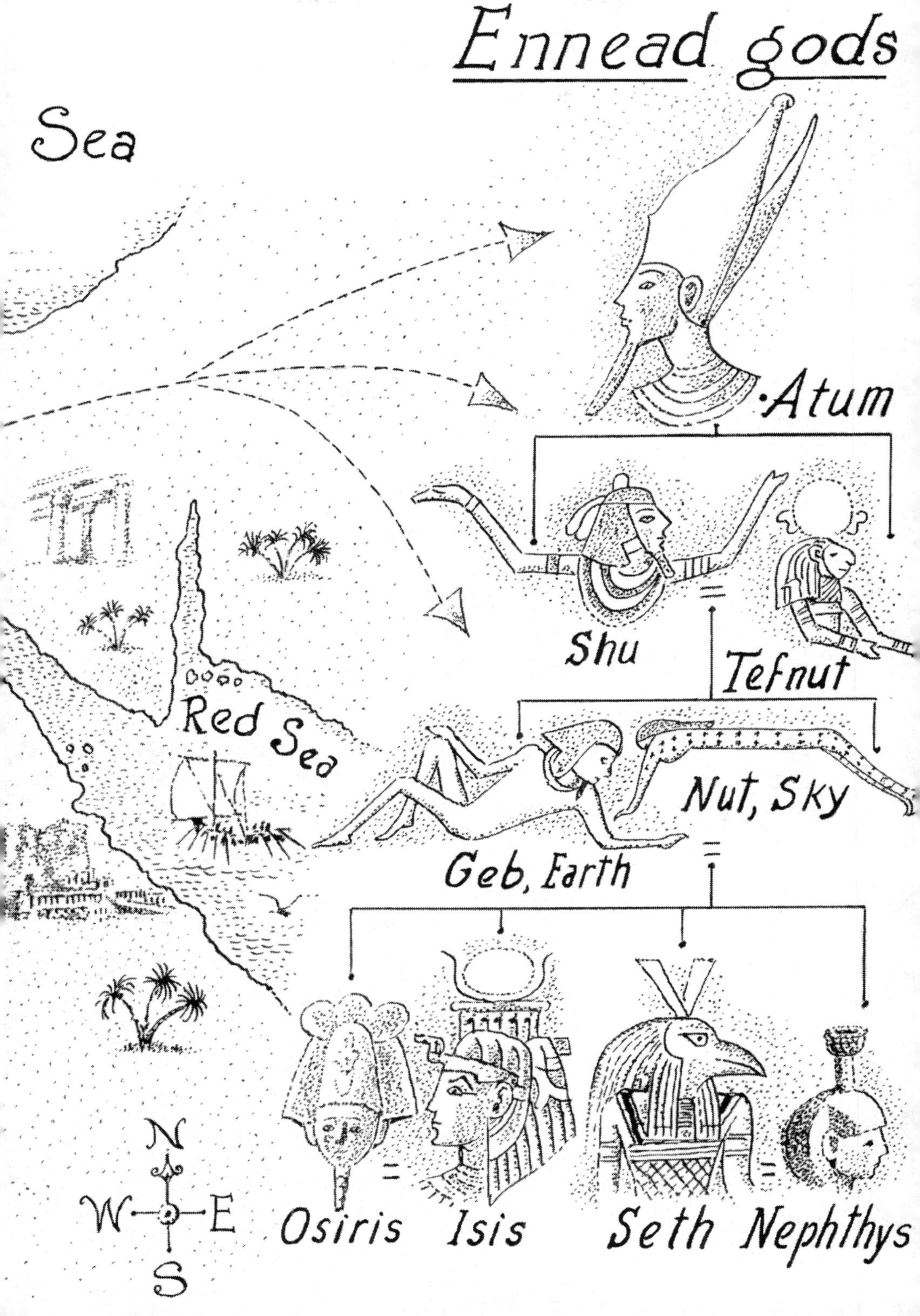
Ennead gods
Sea
Atum
Shu
Tefnut
Red Sea
Nut, Sky
Geb, Earth
Osiris
Isis
Seth
Nephthys
N
W
E
S

## The Land and the Social Pyramid

During these three thousand years, the everyday life of the average Egyptian remained essentially unchanged. Most people were farmers. They were almost completely dependent on the Nile because rainfall was very scarce, and they needed its waters for drinking, cooking, bathing, washing clothes, and irrigating crops. Using barges and boats, they also traveled on the river from city to city.

In addition, the people of Egypt used the Nile to mark the passage of time and the seasons. For example, from June to September, the season they called *akhet*, the Nile flooded, gently covering the fields along its banks with several feet of water and laying down a fresh layer of rich soil. It was not possible to farm the land during this flood season. Many people took the opportunity to rest. Others kept themselves busy making pottery, jewelry, and other handicrafts. Still others worked on government-sponsored projects, including the building of pyramids, temples, and other large stone structures.

Nearly all Egyptians returned to the fields during the other seasons, although a few practiced crafts and trades, such as carpentry and metal-working, year-round. At planting time, in the season of *peret* (lasting from October to February), farmers plowed their fields and planted the seeds of many crops. These included barley, emmer (a kind of wheat), flax (used to make linen cloth), papyrus reeds (used to make paper), and various fruits and vegetables. In the dry season, called *shemu* (lasting from February to June), the farmers harvested these crops. They also raised cattle, goats, sheep, pigs, and other livestock.

A small number of Egyptians were not directly involved in growing food, raising livestock, or the various crafts and trades. Usually, these were wealthier and more socially prominent individuals who ruled over the poorer masses. As noted scholar Lionel Casson explains:

> Egypt's social structure formed a pyramid almost as neat as those built for her kings. It stood foursquare on the broad base of the mass of peasants who cultivated the rich land. Above them rose a series of narrowing layers: the mayors of the villages and their staffs, the governors of the various districts into which the country was divided for administrative purposes and their staffs, the ministers of state and other lofty officials at the capital,and, capstone of the whole, the pharaoh.[3]

The Egyptians looked on the pharaoh as a living god, and he resided, along with his many wives, children, advisors, and noble followers, in great splendor in a large and magnificent palace. There, these elite persons were attended by hundreds of royal servants. Among them were physicians, scribes (who wrote letters and kept records), guards, maids, cooks, bakers, weavers, sculptors, chariot-drivers, and stable-keepers. By contrast, most Egyptian peasants lived in simple huts made of sun-dried bricks. Such humble dwellings typically had one or two small rooms with dirt floors and sometimes housed the owner's animals as well as members of his family.

## Religious Beliefs and Death Rituals

Whether rich or poor, all ancient Egyptians were devoutly religious. They worshiped many gods. In the earliest times, before and during the Early Dynastic Period, each local district (called a *nome*) had its own local god. Later, during the Old Kingdom period, the pharaohs and their chief priests developed a more national religion. This official faith incorporated many, if not most, of the gods, beliefs, and rituals of the local areas. So Egyptian religion, supported by many traditional myths about creation and the gods and their deeds, became quite varied and complex. Moreover, the images, rituals, importance, and authority of many of the gods changed and evolved over the course of many centuries. In this ongoing process, a number of local deities came to be widely worshiped as creator-gods, each of them associated with a different creation myth; and the identities of some gods eventually merged with those of others.[4]

The Egyptians also believed in an afterlife. All hoped that after death they would cross into the Underworld, ruled by the god Osiris, where they would enjoy pleasant lives for eternity. They believed that it was not the physical body, but the soul, that survived after death. In the most common view, the soul was thought to consist of at least two entities, or spirits. The first was the *ka*. This was a person's life force, a sort of guardian angel, which remained with the body in the grave. In contrast, the *ba*, the person's personality, could depart the tomb and ascend into the sky. A common belief was that the stars were the oil lamps of countless numbers of *bas*.[5]

Since the Egyptians believed that the body and part of the soul remained behind in the grave, they viewed burial procedures and customs as vitally important. Those who could afford to erected tombs of brick or stone. The largest and most famous of these stone tombs were, of course, the pyramids, most of which housed royal or noble persons. The Egyptians constructed more than ninety pyramids in all. The two largest are those of the pharaoh Khufu (reigned 2589–2566 B.C.) and his son, Khafra (reigned 2558–2532 B.C.). These massive structures rose on a plateau at Giza, a few miles north of Memphis. The larger one, Khufu's, often called the Great Pyramid, measures about 756 feet on each of the four sides of its base, which covers an area of more than thirteen acres. About 2,300,000 stone blocks, each weighing an average of two-and-one-half tons, went into its construction.[6]

Most Egyptians did not have the luxury of a pyramid to house their bodies. Yet almost everyone observed certain rituals to ensure that they would be able to complete the journey from the land of the living to Osiris's spiritual realm in the Underworld. Among these rituals were preserving the body; burying it in a proper grave; and placing food, clothes, tools, and other items in the grave with the body to sustain the *ka*. For poor Egyptians, the most common practice was to wrap the body in a protective shroud of linen or reeds and place it, along with some meager offerings of food, in a grave dug in the sand.

Those few who could afford it preserved their bodies by mummifying them. After visiting Egypt in the fifth century B.C., the Greek historian Herodotus penned the following account of Egyptian embalmers, those who turned corpses into mummies:

> The kinsmen of the dead man, having agreed upon a price, go away and leave the embalmers to their work. The most perfect process is as follows: as much as possible of the brain is extracted through the nostrils with an iron hook, and what the hook cannot reach is rinsed out with drugs; next the flank [side of the body] is laid open with a flint knife and the whole contents of the abdomen removed; the cavity is then thoroughly cleaned and washed out, first with palm wine and again with . . . pounded spices . . . after which the body is placed in natrum [a mineral salt],covered entirely over, for seventy days—never longer. When this period . . . is over, the body is washed and then wrapped from head to foot in linen cut into strips and smeared on the underside with gum. . . . In this condition the body is given back to the family, who have a wooden case made, shaped like the human figure, into which it is put.[7]

Whether mummified or not, all Egyptians hoped that they would someday find themselves in the presence of Osiris and some of the other immortal gods who played key roles in so many of the popular myths handed down from one generation to another.

# 1

# The Creation of the Gods and Humans

## INTRODUCTION

The creation of the universe, or cosmos, was a central feature of ancient Egyptian religion. A story describing how the cosmos and the things within it came into being is called a cosmogony (whereas the study of the nature and structure of the created cosmos is referred to as a cosmology). The Egyptians had several different cosmogonies that coexisted and complemented one another. This may seem strange to modern Christians, Jews, and Muslims, who are used to a single creation story.

A major reason that the Egyptians had so many creation myths is that their religion was local in character. "Each town or area," says Northern Arizona University scholar Eugene Cruz-Uribe, "had a patron deity, and the local temple physically occupied the site where the creation was supposed to have taken place. Thus, each town potentially could have its own creation myth in which the local god was the creator."[1] The country's various regions, therefore, developed very strong local religious traditions.

On the national level, the kings, known as pharaohs, wisely understood that recognizing all of these local traditions was a way of keeping loyalty and order. According to Egyptologist Leonard H. Lesko of Brown University, "Gradually, or perhaps quickly, local myths from throughout the country were brought together into a system . . . which sought to include almost every god and thereby to satisfy almost every person."[2]

There were four major Egyptian cosmogonies (along with a number of minor ones), each associated with the city or geographic area where it originated. One came from Heliopolis, the "City of the Sun," located on the site of Egypt's modern capital, Cairo. The creator god of the Heliopolis area was Atum, the "lord to the limits of the sky." Atum was thought to have given rise to eight other gods: Shu, Tefnut, Geb, Nut, Osiris, Seth, Isis, and Nephthys. These eight deities, along with Atum himself, were referred to collectively as the sacred Ennead, a word that means a group of nine.

At Memphis (about fifteen miles south of Heliopolis, or Cairo), ancient Egypt's earliest national capital, the creation story centered instead around the god Ptah. The Memphite priests believed that Ptah was so powerful that he was able to create the members of the sacred Ennead, including Atum, simply by pronouncing their names.

By contrast, at Hermopolis, about one hundred fifty miles south of Memphis, the principal creation story involved a different group of gods. This group—the Ogdoad (a word similar to *octet*, or group of eight)—had eight members: Nu, Naunet, Hey, Hauhet, Kek, Kauket, Amun, and Amaunet. The priests at Hermopolis believed that these deities gave rise to Atum, who went on to create humans and animals.

Finally, at Thebes, an important city situated a few hundred miles from Hermopolis, the priests singled out Amun, one of the Ogdoad. Thought by the Theban priests to have predated the other members of the Ogdoad, Amun became known to the local people as the "First One who gave birth to the first ones."

It is important to realize that the Egyptians eventually recognized and worshiped all of these gods and came to view the various creation stories as equally valid. Although the local traditions conflicted with one another in certain ways, they also shared certain concepts, gods, and events. This was especially true of the Theban version, told below, which attempted to gain credence by incorporating elements of the other three cosmogonies and associating all other creator gods with Amun. Thus, Amun fulfills the same basic "creator" role in the Theban cosmogony that Atum does in the Heliopolis cosmogony and that Ptah does in the Memphis cosmogony. And the Theban cosmogony recognizes and incorporates the eight gods of the Ogdoad of Hermopolis; the main difference is that in the Hermopolitan version Amun is merely one of the eight, while in the Theban version he is the first and creates the other seven. Similarly, the Theban version recognizes the nine gods of the Ennead sacred at Heliopolis and Memphis, but claims that Amun, rather than Atum or Ptah, created them.

The surviving original sources describing these Egyptian gods and creation stories vary in character. Many take the form of inscriptions (words and pictures carved into stone) on the walls of temples. Fragments of these stories also appear in inscriptions, paintings, and writings found in tombs and graves. For example, between about 2350 and 2150 B.C. priests carved a series of spells and incantations inside the pyramid tombs of the pharaohs, hoping to ensure their safe passage into the afterlife.[3] These carvings, now called the *Pyramid Texts*, reveal a good deal of information about the gods and their myths.

Later, between about 2040 and 1780 B.C., descriptions of divine matters were painted on the caskets of Egyptian nobles; so they are referred to, rather appropriately, as the *Coffin Texts*.

Later still, some burials included similar funerary texts written on scrolls made of papyrus (an early form of paper), perhaps the most famous being the *Book of the Dead*.

The *Book of the Dead* is actually a term coined by modern researchers. The ancient Egyptians called it the "spell for coming forth by day." It consisted of about two hundred magical spells, many of which were taken from the *Pyramid* and *Coffin Texts*. Spell number 125 is among the most famous. It was usually accompanied by a brief interaction between a deceased person, the god Osiris, and the god's subordinate judges. In the judgment procedure conducted by these deities, the person "confessed" that he or she had not lied, stolen, or committed other crimes and misdemeanors. If Osiris and his judges found the person "true of voice," they allowed him or her to enter the realm of the dead. This and other portions of the *Book of the Dead* were important elements in the complex religious mythology that gave birth to the colorful stories that follow.

## THE CREATION OF THE GODS AND HUMANS

### How the Gods Came To Be

In the beginning, there was only chaos, which stretched, dark and silent, throughout all space and eternity. Later, people in some parts of Egypt came to see this bottomless abyss containing a limitless ocean of black, lifeless water as a living being. They called the nothingness Nu and worshiped him as a god. Whatever one chooses to call this dismal and foreboding state of nonexistence, a time came, long ago, when a dramatic and wonderful event transformed nonexistence into existence. This was the creation of Amun, the First One, the King of the Gods, the maker of all things. No other god was needed to make him. Indeed, because he had no father or mother, Amun somehow created himself, in an invisible, secret way that no human being has ever known or will ever discover.

As Amun mysteriously sprang into being, the deathly stillness of the cosmos was shattered by his magnificent piercing voice. This mighty blast set in motion all the rest of creation. In some parts of Egypt people believed that in this early stage of his existence Amun took the form of a gigantic goose, the Great Honker. He certainly went on to assume many other forms, as his will and needs dictated.

The first of the forms Amun took was that of one part of the Ogdoad, the group of eight gods that later became sacred to the priests at Hermopolis. These priests claimed that the eight earliest gods (Nu, Naunet, Hey, Hauhet, Kek, Kauket, Amun, and Amaunet), who had the heads of frogs and serpents, swam through the dark waters of chaos. By contrast, the priests at Thebes said that first the mighty Amun created the other seven and then joined them as the eighth member of the Ogdoad.

Next, said the Theban priests, Amun took the form of the first dry land. On this so-called primeval mound he proceeded to create the Ennead, the group of nine gods that later became sacred to the priests at Heliopolis and Memphis. These included Atum, Shu, Tefnut, Geb, Nut, Osiris, Seth, Isis, and Nephthys. At this time, Amun also created the ram-headed god Khnum and all the other gods, spirits, and demons that inhabit the sky, earth, and Underworld. In addition, in the center of the primeval mound Amun shaped the first city—sacred Thebes—where at first many of the gods made their home.

## The Rise of Humans, Cities, Animals, and Plants

After these strenuous acts of creation, Amun rose into the sky and assumed the shape and features of the life-giving sun (in which form he is often called Amun-Ra). As he looked down from above, a new phase of creation began, namely that of the earth and the humans that inhabit it. To complete this task, Amun chose the ram-headed god Khnum, whom the Egyptians came to call, along with Amun, one of the two Lords of Destiny. The destiny Khnum controlled was that of the human race. He proceeded, with Amun's blessing, to model the first humans on his divine potter's wheel.

Khnum began by fashioning the bones from a special clay. Over this inner frame he molded skin, veins carrying blood, and various organs, including those for digestion, breathing, and having children. He gave the bodies of the first humans all the elements and details familiar in human bodies today. But though the physical forms were complete, they did not yet possess the sparks of life, including movement and thought. So Khnum breathed into his creations, passing them some of his own life force and thereby animating them.

Immediately it became clear that these new creatures Khnum had created would need someplace to live. With the aid of Amun on high, Khnum rolled back the dark waters surrounding the primeval mound, thus exposing more dry land. And on this new land he helped the first people to establish new cities, most of them modeled on the plan of sacred Thebes. Khnum also populated the new land, which became known as Egypt, with all manner of living beasts, from birds, to fish, to crocodiles, to beetles; and he made trees, crops, and other plants grow in abundance on the face of the earth. In time, as the humans had their own children and multiplied, other more distant lands became populated. But Egypt remained the center of the world shaped by Amun and the gods he himself had created.

# QUESTIONS AND ANSWERS

**Q:** *What is a cosmogony?*

**A:** A cosmogony is a story telling how the cosmos, and the things in it, came into being.

**Q:** *What features do the various Egyptian creation myths have in common?*

**A:** First, they all picture a time before the gods existed, identified variously as chaos, a void or bottomless abyss (pit), a dark ocean, or some combination of these. Sometimes people envisioned this pre-creation state as a living force and gave it a name; at Heliopolis, for instance, they called it Nu (or Nun). Typically, the cosmogonies also feature a primeval mound of earth, the *Ta-tenen*, on which a creator god stood and the first city rose. Many modern experts believe that the pyramids the Egyptians built as tombs were supposed to be symbolic representations of this first hill (although others think the pyramids were meant to represent a sort of stairway to heaven).

**Q:** *According to the Theban creation myth, what force shattered the cosmos's original quiet, state?*

**A:** Amun's powerful voice was a blast of sound that signaled the beginning of the first round of creation.

**Q:** *In the Theban cosmogony, what are the two sacred groups of gods that Amun creates, and of which group is he himself a member?*

**A:** He creates the Ennead, made up of nine gods, and the Ogdoad, a group of eight gods. Amun is a member of the Ogdoad.

**Q:** *How does the ram-headed god Khnum fashion human beings?*

**A:** He creates them from clay, which he molds on his potter's wheel. Then he breathes life into them, allowing them to move, think, talk, and so forth. The idea of humans being created from clay or dirt is a common theme in the religious myths of many peoples. For instance, in one of the ancient Greek creation myths, the god Prometheus fashions humans from clay. Similarly, in the Judeo-Christian Bible, God makes the first man, Adam, from dust.

**Q:** *According to the Theban cosmogony, what was the model the first humans used for the cities they built?*

**A:** Their model was the sacred city of Thebes, constructed by Amun in the center of the primeval mound of creation.

# EXPERT COMMENTARY

One major difference between the ancient Egyptians and many people in the United States and other modern Western countries is that most Egyptians accepted without question the authenticity of their gods and the creation myths surrounding them, whereas large numbers of Westerners view their own creation stories as mere fables. Byron E. Shafer, an associate professor of religious studies at Fordham University, explains this and other important differences:

> As ancient Egyptian artistry is immediately satisfying to modern Western observers, so ancient Egyptian religion is immediately puzzling. Many people today, though undoubtedly concerned with the problem of life's meaning, are agnostics [those who admit God might exist but see no proof for it] or atheists [those who reject outright the existence of God]; very few such people could be found among the ancient Egyptians. Many people today find life's meaning outside of religion and view religion as incidental or tangential to [a minor aspect of] life; very few ancient Egyptians saw it this way. Of today's devout, all but a few are monotheists [believers in a single god]; of ancient Egypt's, all but a few were polytheists [believers in many gods]. . . . We hold omnipotence [having all power] and omniscience [having all knowledge] as necessary attributes of divinity; they did not. We have a cannon of scripture [such as the Bible or Koran]; they did not. We reject magic; they did not. We view government as secular [nonreligious] and rulers as all too human; they saw government as sacred and kings as somehow divine. We believe that the world needs to be improved, and therefore (if we are religious) to be transformed by communal obedience to God's revealed will; they believed that the world needs to be maintained, and therefore to be stabilized by governmental imposition of order from above.[4]

In the following excerpt from his book on Egyptian myths, George Hart, of the British Museum and University of London, considers a possible link between the creation myth of Khnum and a well-known Greek creation story:

> It has been suggested that the idea of Khnum molding a human being on the potter's wheel, which goes far back in Egypt in [sculpted] relief and inscriptions . . . could have influenced the traditions that the

Greek poet Hesiod (ca. 700 B.C.) drew upon for the making of Pandora, which he describes both in his *Theogony and Works and Days*. There, Zeus [the chief Greek god] instructed Hephaestos [god of fire and metalworking] to mold a woman, Pandora, out of clay, who would bring mankind limitless miseries. But it is quite probable that the Hesiodic concept of Pandora is an independent tradition—certainly the malicious [mean and harmful] intentions of Zeus are far from the spirit of the philanthropic [charitable] Khnum.[5]

# 2

# The Murder of Osiris

## INTRODUCTION

Osiris was one of the most important of all the Egyptian gods. According to the Heliopolitan version of the creation, he was the son of the deities Nut and Geb. Along with them, he numbered among the nine gods who formed the sacred Ennead. At first, Osiris was a fertility god associated with vegetation and the rich soil of the Nile delta. In time, however, he came to be seen as the ruler of the Underworld.[1] He was also both the brother and husband of Isis, another member of the Ennead. The royal families of the ancient Egyptians did not feel constrained by the taboos against incest—sexual relations between close relatives—that most modern peoples do. The idea of Osiris and Isis marrying and giving birth to a son was seen by these rulers as both the justification and the model for such royal brother-sister marriages, which became common in many ancient civilizations.

In their paintings, the Egyptians most often pictured Osiris as a mummy wrapped in bandages, but with his hands free and holding the crook and flail, the chief insignia of Egyptian royalty. The crook was a royal scepter shaped like a hook; the flail was a stick with long tassels hanging from one end. Sometimes in these paintings Osiris's head is topped by rams' horns, but more often he wears the *atef*, a white crown shaped somewhat like a bowling pin with a plume attached to either side. His skin is either white, black, or green, the latter being the color associated with resurrection, or rebirth.

Indeed, in the chief myth about Osiris he is murdered but later undergoes a Christ-like resurrection. This story was central to the religious worship of the Egyptians, as well as to the succession and rule of the pharaohs in Egypt. The combination of the god's fertility and his image as the controller of the Underworld, or the world of the dead, was seen as an extremely potent force. By at least 2400 B.C., a dead king was identified with and believed even to take on the guise (spirit and powers) of Osiris; while the new king who took his place came to be identified with Osiris's son, Horus. The Egyptians viewed this human identification with the divine as the noblest example of the endless cycle of death and renewal that they perceived everywhere in the natural world. The theme of birth, death, and rebirth was one of the pillars of Egyptian religion.

Parts of Osiris's story were discovered on various ancient Egyptian papyri and stone carvings. However, the most complete version is a much later one preserved around A.D. 100 by the Greek writer Plutarch in his story *Concerning Isis and Osiris*. (Egyptian and other Near Eastern stories were often retold later by the Greeks and Romans.) Besides Osiris, his sister (and wife) Isis, and their son, Horus, the other main characters are Osiris's brother Seth and sister Nephthys.

## THE MURDER OF OSIRIS

### Seth Overcomes Osiris

There was once a golden age in which the people of Egypt lived in a state of prosperity and happiness. By order of the sun god Ra, the kindly god Osiris ruled the land as king. Osiris's sister, the goddess Isis, sat at his side as his wife and Egypt's beautiful, wise, and strong-willed queen. Osiris was indeed a kind and helpful king. He showed the people how to plant crops and to irrigate them using the waters that were so plentiful when the Nile River overflowed its banks each year. He also instructed them in making laws and worshiping the gods in the proper manner. Eventually, the god-king went on a long pilgrimage to bring these same gifts of civilization to the inhabitants of other lands.

While Osiris was away, Isis ruled Egypt in his stead. She kept a watchful eye on their brother Seth because she sensed that Seth felt jealousy and hatred for Osiris, and she feared that Seth might be scheming to steal his brother's throne. Indeed, Seth was planning to overthrow Osiris, but for the present he bode his time, waiting for the right opportunity to strike. And when Osiris returned from his journey, Seth pretended to be pleased to see him.

Seth's big chance came at last when Isis was away on a short trip and Osiris invited him to attend a lavish banquet at the palace. Arriving at the party, Seth put on a friendly face and circulated among the guests, bragging repeatedly about a beautifully decorated chest that someone had recently built for him. He even had some servants bring the chest to the party, and everyone, including Osiris, was duly impressed with its fine craftsmanship.

After all those present had downed a great deal of wine, Seth sprang his trap. "I'd like to offer the following challenge," he said. "Each of you can take turns lying down inside the chest, and the first person who fits in it exactly will receive it as my gift!" Eager to own such a magnificent treasure, each guest took a turn lying in the chest, but no one fit in it exactly right. Finally, Osiris climbed in. He had no idea, of course, that Seth had purposely commissioned the box to fit Osiris's god-like measurements. "Ah!" Osiris happily exclaimed. "See, Seth, how well I fit in here. I'll wager that when you issued your challenge you never expected you'd have to give the chest to me!"

"To the contrary," Seth chortled with an evil grin. "The chest is now yours, brother, forever!" Then, suddenly, Seth slammed down the lid, trapping Osiris inside. And while his servants held back the other guests, Seth poured melted lead over the chest, sealing it and killing poor Osiris. The conspirators then carried the box, which was now a coffin, to the Nile and threw it in. Seth roared in triumph, "Finally, I have rid myself of that worthless do-gooder and can enjoy what Ra should have given me in the first place!" Then Seth declared himself the new king of Egypt.

## Isis Searches for Her Husband

When Isis returned, she learned of the tragedy that had befallen her husband, as well as the kingdom, which was now under the rule of an evil monarch. Naturally, she was both shocked and grief-stricken. After cutting her hair and donning black garments in the traditional Egyptian manner of mourning, she immediately set out to find Osiris's body. She wanted to give it a proper funeral, for the dead would not rest peacefully without certain necessary funeral rituals. Isis searched every inch of the Nile in the area in which the murderers had dumped the chest, but by then, she realized, it had floated out to sea. Calculating the prevailing ocean currents to be northerly, Isis left Egypt and journeyed in a horse-drawn cart up the coast of Palestine (the land to the northeast of Egypt), searching for a floating box and asking everyone she met if they had seen one.

Eventually, Isis learned that such a chest had floated ashore near the port city of Byblos (north of Palestine), where it had come to rest among the exposed roots of a small young tree. Even in death Osiris's body retained its strong powers of fertility. As if by a miracle, the tree on which his chest had landed had grown to its full size overnight, enveloping the chest inside its massive new trunk. Hearing of this singular event, the local king had ordered the tree cut down and brought to his palace to be used as a pillar. He had no idea that a god's remains rested inside the tree's massive trunk.

But when she heard the local people tell the story of the miraculous tree, Isis knew what must have happened. Cleverly, she disguised herself as a simple hairdresser and managed to gain entrance to the palace. There, she gained the confidence of the king and queen to such a degree that they asked her to watch over their own child. Each night, when everyone had gone to bed, the goddess would go to the pillar in which her beloved husband's body rested and quietly weep.

In time, she decided to reveal her true divine nature to the royal couple. When the king and queen heard that the god Osiris was trapped inside their pillar, they quickly ordered it cut open. Inside, still intact, was Osiris's chest containing his remains. They presented the chest to Isis, who carried it in her cart back to Egypt. For many centuries to come, what remained of the pillar that had harbored the dead god was preserved and worshiped in Byblos.

## Resurrection and the Conquest of Death

Once back in Egypt, Isis carefully avoided towns and other crowded places so that word would not reach Seth that she had arrived home with Osiris's remains. In a secret, desolate place, she used some sharp metal tools to unseal the casket, and she gazed once again on the face of her husband, who appeared to be merely asleep. Sobbing almost uncontrollably, she embraced him and then resealed the box. For a while, she kept a silent vigil over it, guarding it from harm.

One night, when Seth was out hunting birds in the Nile marshes, he stumbled on the coffin, which Isis had hidden among the rushes. The new god-king, who ruled his people harshly, immediately recognized this coffin as the chest bearing his dead brother. Seeing that Isis was asleep nearby, Seth quietly opened the box, removed the corpse, and carried it far away. "Now I'll destroy you completely, as I should have done before!" Seth said, and he angrily cut and tore Osiris's body into many pieces. After he had done this grisly deed, he had his servants hide the pieces all across the land of Egypt. He was certain that Isis would have no chance of finding them all.

But Seth had again underestimated his sister's powers. With the help of Nephthys, Seth's wife (who loved Isis and Osiris more than she loved her evil husband), Isis searched relentlessly for the scattered shreds of her husband's body. After many years, the two women found all the hidden pieces, and Isis was able, with great difficulty, to piece Osiris back together. Using every magic spell she could remember, she managed to bring him back to life for a single night. The two declared their undying love for each other. And that night they conceived a son, Horus.

The next morning Osiris departed the earth forever. Though he was now truly dead, he had in a sense conquered death, for the mighty Ra proceeded to make him lord of the Underworld. And from that day forward, no Egyptian ever again feared death, knowing that his or her spirit would be well cared for in the peaceful realm that Osiris now ruled.

# QUESTIONS AND ANSWERS

***Q:*** *Although Osiris and Isis were gods, they were often subject to the wishes and powers of someone higher. Who was it?*

***A:*** Ra, the sun god.

***Q:*** *Why did Seth scheme against his brother Osiris?*

***A:*** Seth was jealous because Ra, the sun god, had made Osiris the ruler of Egypt, and Seth wanted the job for himself.

***Q:*** *How did Seth trick Osiris into climbing into the chest?*

***A:*** Seth promised to give the chest as a gift to whoever fit into it perfectly.

***Q:*** *How was the tree on whose roots Osiris's chest landed able to grow so large in a single night?*

***A:*** Osiris had the power of fertility, so he was able to make plants and animals grow quickly and healthily.

***Q:*** *In the story of Osiris's resurrection, what were two major signs that Osiris had the power to renew life?*

***A:*** First, he was reborn from the dead. Second, he managed to create a son—Horus.

***Q:*** *What role did Isis play in helping her husband achieve renewed life?*

***A:*** First, Isis was both loyal and persistent. She never gave up hope of finding Osiris, and when she did find him she patiently tended his body, making sure to piece it back together after Seth cut it up. Also, the power of her love helped Osiris to regain momentary life.

# EXPERT COMMENTARY

Brown University scholar Leonard Lesko comments here on some of the nonreligious themes in the myth of Osiris's murder and resurrection:

> On one level of meaning, the struggle between Osiris and Seth represents a conflict in nature—between the fertile Nile Valley (Kemet, the black land) and the infertile desert (Deshret, the red land) or between the consistent,beneficial inundation [flooding] of the Nile (Osiris) and the unpredictable, generally undesirable storm (Seth). On another level, reflected in later texts, the struggle represents a conflict between two . . . heirs contending for the rule of their father, the earth, clearly symbolizing the struggle between kings of the north and south for control of the country [since Egypt was once divided into lower and upper kingdoms before King Menes unified them around 3000 B.C.].[2]

The mystical and religious significance of Osiris's myth to ordinary ancient Egyptians was that it promised renewal, specifically the negation of death and attainment of eternal life, as the University of Cologne's Philippe Derchain explains:

> Whoever identified himself with Osiris identified himself with the forces of renewal in the universe. . . . The dead man survives not because he has a son alive on earth but because he has been integrated into the generalized scheme of father-son relationships [as shown by the relationship between Osiris and Horus in the myth]. . . . Human destiny. . . is projected as a cyclical [constantly repeating] phenomenon. . . in which the individual finds his salvation. Moreover, every periodic [cyclical or repeating] phenomenon could serve as the model of a myth of the negation of death [just as Osiris conquers death in his myth], such as the daily course of the sun. To reach the boat of the sun and sail with it was originally the privilege of the king alone. . . . Later the sun would take everybody on board, so that people would commonly refer to the boat as the "boat of millions." This is one of the doctrines that formed the basis of the *Book of the Dead*.[3]

Noted journalist and historian Paul Johnson here comments on the historical aspects of the Osiris legend:

The story very likely had a historical origin germane to Egypt's actual formation, but in Egyptian theology and ritual it was presented as a recurring life-cycle, with the Horus-king struggling with the forces of evil during his life, and becoming Osiris, and immortal, in death. Originally only the pharaoh enacted this cyclical drama but from the late Old Kingdom onwards the right to struggle with Seth and be immortalized with Osiris was gradually extended to all Egyptians. The universalizing of the myth accompanied the historical development of the individual conscience, Egypt's greatest spiritual gift to mankind, and to the idea of a last judgment for all, presided over by Osiris.[4]

# 3

# ISIS AND THE SEVEN SCORPIONS

## INTRODUCTION

The Egyptians viewed Isis not only as Osiris's loyal sister and wife, but also as a devoted mother-figure who watched over and protected her son, Horus, and, by extension, all children. Isis also had a reputation as a powerful healer who could cure people through her use of magic. "Her magic was allied to the wisdom of Thoth [god of wisdom and writing]," explains scholar Richard Patrick, "and given to mankind as a skill in healing."[1] Thus, several of the stories associated with her were told and retold to show people the specific healing spells they would need to cure various ailments, ranging from fevers to animal bites.

Often, these cures were collected in medical manuals (written on papyrus) and when someone was sick, the healer consulted the appropriate manual. For example, a person with a fever or a burn was seen to assume temporarily the role of Horus, Isis's son, while the healer represented Isis. The healer recited the correct spell over a bowl containing a mixture of human milk, gum, and cat hairs, and then rubbed the coarse ointment onto the patient, who usually felt some relief.[2]

The myth of Isis and the Seven Scorpions, which follows, neatly combines these two images of the goddess: mother and magic healer. The reason that there are seven scorpions in the story, and not some other number, is probably that the number seven had mystical significance in the lore of many ancient societies, including that of Egypt. The Egyptians saw seven as having tremendous potency and strength. (Therefore, the number appeared in many medical cures; for example, a standard spell to relieve headaches involved the tying of seven knots.) The principal source for the story is the Metternich stele, an inscribed stone used as a marker or monument, discovered in Alexandria, Egypt in 1828. The inscriptions on the Metternich stele also include episodes about the lives of various other gods.[3]

In this story, the main characters are Isis; Thoth, the god of wisdom and writing; the seven scorpions; and two Egyptian women.

## ISIS AND THE SEVEN SCORPIONS

### Isis Flees From Seth

After Seth had killed Osiris, Isis had given birth to her son, Horus, and the sun god Ra had made Osiris lord of the Underworld, Isis began weaving a shroud to place around her husband's mummy. Despite the fact that Osiris's spirit now reigned beneath the horizon, his lifeless body still required preparation for burial, as well as burial itself. The infant Horus lay in a crib beside Isis as she worked. Soon Thoth, the god of wisdom, approached the new mother and warned, "Take care, Isis. Seth is looking for you and your son. I fear he means to kill you both."

"I must protect my son at all costs," she said. "That is my primary task, since I am his mother. But what can I do? Where can I hide? Seth knows every rock, cave, and bush for miles around. He is sure to find us."

Thoth told Isis not to despair. He pointed out that Seth was unfamiliar with certain marshes located far to the north in the Nile delta, and that if she and Horus hid there Seth would not be able to find them. "Go there," Thoth urged, "raise Horus well, and when he is old enough, he can return to avenge Osiris and take the throne from Seth."

Isis followed Thoth's instructions. Before he departed, Thoth left seven huge scorpions to accompany and protect Isis and her son on their perilous journey. Three of the scorpions—Petet, Tjetet, and Matet—walked along in front of Isis, keeping a wary eye out for Seth or any other threatening presences; two more scorpions, Mesetet and Mesetetef, positioned themselves under her cart; while the other two, Tefen and Befen, guarded the rear. Luckily, the travelers did not encounter any trouble during the trip.

## The Scorpions' Revenge

Eventually, the party neared the delta region that Thoth had recommended as a hiding place. By this time, the loving mother, still cradling her baby, was exhausted and desperately in need of food and rest. They came to a village, and there they approached a large, splendid-looking house, hoping that the owner might offer them hospitality. At that very moment, the owner, a woman dressed in fine clothes, was standing in her doorway. However, when she caught sight of the seven scorpions, she became terrified and slammed the door, refusing any help to the mother and child.

Disappointed and forlorn, Isis decided that there was nothing she could do but continue on toward the marshes. She had walked on a few hundred feet, when to her surprise a poor fisherman's daughter approached her. The girl did not recognize Isis as a goddess and, though she kept a cautious eye on the scorpions, she did not shy away. "I could not help but notice how tired and hungry you look," said the girl in a kindly voice.

"Please, you must come with me to my house and let me give you and your child something to eat." Then the girl led Isis to a tiny, spare, one-room hut and there gave her most of what little food she had.

Meanwhile, the scorpions were angry at the rich woman who had so rudely refused to help Isis and her son. Therefore, they decided to teach the woman a hard lesson. Tefen raised up his stinger, and his six companions loaded their poisons onto it. Then he stealthily crept under the rich woman's door, found where her young son was sleeping, and stung him. Just as the boy's mother was entering the room, Tefen scurried away.

Distraught, the woman carried her child's limp, swollen body through the streets, desperately seeking help. But everyone was afraid of the scorpions and their poison, and all the townspeople shut their doors in her face, just as she had recently done to another mother and son in need. Sobbing, the woman sank to the ground, cradling the boy's body in her arms.

## The Power of Isis's Magic

Isis soon learned what had happened. Despite having been treated so rudely, she could not bear to allow an innocent child to die and its mother to suffer so cruelly. So Isis went to the rich woman and said, "Fear not. I am the goddess Isis. Give me your son and I will heal him." Overcome with awe, the woman quickly handed over the boy, and Isis held him tenderly. The goddess then proceeded to recite various spells, in the process naming each of the seven scorpions, and thereby establishing her power over them and their poisons.

For several moments a great hush gripped the village as everyone peeked out from their houses to watch the drama unfolding in the street. At first, the boy's body remained limp and pale. But then, little by little, his color began to return, his breathing became normal, and he opened his eyes. Recognizing his mother, he reached out for her, and Isis delivered him into her arms. The rich woman thanked the goddess, but seemed to sense that words were not enough to repay the kindness Isis had done. Without hesitation, the woman returned home, gathered a major portion of her gold, jewels, and other wealth, carried the treasure to the poor fisherman's hut, and bestowed it on the poor young girl who had earlier helped the goddess.

In the end, things worked out well for everyone involved: Isis went on to avoid Seth and to raise Horus. The fisherman's daughter enjoyed material comforts she would otherwise never have known. And the rich woman, who was now considerably less rich than before, learned the true value of kindness and hospitality.

# QUESTIONS AND ANSWERS

**Q:** *Why did Isis need to leave her home?*

**A:** Thoth, the god of wisdom, warned the goddess that Seth, the evil pharaoh, meant to kill her and her infant son, Horus.

**Q:** *Where did Thoth advise Isis to go?*

**A:** He advised her to hide in the marshes located near the Nile delta.

**Q:** *Why did Thoth give Isis the scorpions?*

**A:** Thoth gave them to Isis to protect her and Horus from danger on their journey.

**Q:** *Why were there seven scorpions in the myth instead of five, nine, or some other number?*

**A:** To the Egyptians (as well as to many other ancient peoples), the number seven had mystical significance and special powers.

**Q:** *Why did the rich woman refuse to help Isis and her child?*

**A:** She was afraid of the seven scorpions.

**Q:** *How did the scorpion named Tefen get into the rich woman's house, and what did he do once he was inside?*

**A:** Tefen crawled under the door. Once inside, he stung the woman's sleeping son, making him gravely ill.

**Q:** *What special powers did Isis display in this story?*

**A:** The power to heal, and the power to forgive and be compassionate.

**Q:** *How did Isis gain power over the scorpions in order to cure the boy?*

**A:** She named them, one by one. Many ancient peoples, including the Egyptians, believed that gods could create something or exercise their power in other ways through the mere act of speech.

**Q:** *What did the rich woman learn as a result of Isis's kindness?*

**A:** The rich woman learned the true value of hospitality. She came to realize that if she had just been kind to Isis and shown her hospitality in the first place, she would not have brought down the vengeance of the scorpions on herself and her innocent son. The lesson of the story, therefore, is that showing kindness brings kindness in return, while rudeness causes only hard feelings and hostility.

# EXPERT COMMENTARY

Isis was the Egyptian version of the "Great Mother" character who is present in the mythologies of many different peoples and with whom women in any culture could easily identify. According to British mythologist Donald Mackenzie:

> The typical Great Mother was a virgin goddess who represented the female principle [i.e., the traditional attributes of women]. . . . The characteristics of the several different mother deities varied in different localities. . . . One Great Mother was an earth spirit, another was a water spirit, and a third was an atmosphere or sky spirit. . . . The popular Isis ultimately combined the attributes of all the Great Mothers, who [in Egyptian eyes] were regarded as different manifestations of her.[4]

No better expert on Isis exists than Isis herself, at least the goddess as she is portrayed in the novel *The Golden Ass*, by the second-century A.D. Roman writer, Apuleius. By his day, the worship of Isis had spread throughout the Mediterranean world and was extremely popular in both Greece and Rome. The Greeks and Romans viewed her as a sort of universal goddess with a wide range of attributes and all-encompassing powers. In this excerpt from the novel, the hero, who has just prayed to Isis for help, sees her miraculously materialize before him. "Here I am, Lucius," she says,

> roused by your prayers. I am the mother of the world of nature, mistress of all the elements, first-born in this realm of time. I am the loftiest of Deities, queen of departed spirits, foremost of heavenly dwellers, the single embodiment of all the gods and goddesses. I order with my nod the luminous heights of heaven, the healthy sea-breezes, the sad silences of the infernal dwellers [i.e., those in the Underworld]. The whole world worships this single godhead under a variety of shapes and... titles.... But the Egyptians... call me by my true name, which is Queen Isis.[5]

Lionel Casson, one of the twentieth century's greatest scholars of ancient societies, explains why Isis was so extremely popular among the Romans (and their Greek subjects):

The first century B.C. and the several centuries that followed, was an age in which people throughout the Mediterranean world were in desperate search of a religious experience that could offer them some hope and comfort. The story of. . . Isis, the wife who by her unswerving faith and love had made the resurrection [of Osiris] possible. . . proved to possess universal appeal. The emphasis on immortality in the worship of [Isis and Osiris] gained numerous devotees throughout the length and breadth of the Roman Empire, from the ancient Near East to far-off Britain.[6]

# 4

# The Revenge of Horus

## INTRODUCTION

The death of Osiris and his later resurrection as the lord of the Underworld constitute the first half of what is sometimes called the Myth of Kingship. The story of Osiris explains why an Egyptian pharaoh "became" this god-king when he died. The second part of the Myth of Kingship tells the story of Osiris's son, Horus, whom a pharaoh in a sense "became," or with whom he at least identified, while he was alive and ruling Egypt.

Horus became known as the "Avenger" because in his most famous myth, which is told here, he avenged the death of his father, Osiris. Horus was also often called the "Far-Above-One," because people usually pictured him as a sky god in the form of a hawk soaring above the earth. Surviving Egyptian statues and paintings frequently show him as a magnificent bird who wears Egypt's white crown (the *atef*), which symbolizes his association with the living god-king, or pharaoh.

Over the centuries, Horus took on many manifestations (guises or identities). This is because worshipers at different times and places in Egypt's history emphasized different aspects of his character. But his most important identity was always that of Osiris's son. "Horus, son of Isis and Osiris," says scholar Lewis Spence, "was regarded as of such importance that he absorbed the attributes of all the other Horus-gods."[1] In this identity, Horus was part of what became known as the "Triad of Abydos." A triad is a group of three, and in this case the sacred three were Osiris, Isis, and their son, Horus. Abydos was a city located on the Nile northwest of Thebes, and the ruins of its main temple house some of the most important artistic renderings of the events of Horus's principal myth.

Horus and his principal myth, in which Seth briefly takes the form of a hippopotamus, also figured prominently in the art and culture of other Egyptian cities. For example, at ancient Edfu, on the Nile's west bank several miles south of Thebes, a yearly religious celebration—the festival of victory—featured a sort of play. Actors portrayed Seth as a hippopotamus and Horus and Isis harpooning him. The Seth/hippo was speared over and over, and eventually replicas of his limbs and organs were sacrificed to various gods. At the conclusion of the festival, worshipers ate hippopotamus cakes, symbolizing Seth's total destruction.[2]

Besides Horus and his parents, Osiris and Isis, the myth features many other characters. Among these are the chief god, the sun deity Ra; Thoth, god of wisdom and writing; Neith, an early creator-goddess worshiped in the Nile delta; Nemty, a ferryman; Hathor, a sky-goddess who later became closely associated with Horus; and Seth, the brother of Osiris and Isis, who had earlier attacked and killed Osiris.

## THE REVENGE OF HORUS

### Horus Challenges Seth

After he had killed Osiris and ascended to Egypt's throne, Seth expected to reign for a very long time. As it turned out, however, he was sorely mistaken. Seth had not reckoned on the birth of Horus or foreseen that this son of his brother Osiris and his sister Isis would come to challenge his uncle for mastery of the lands of the Nile. Indeed, this is exactly the course of action Horus pursued when he grew old enough. First, he summoned the gods of the sacred Ennead, along with a number of other deities, and asked them to sit in judgment, reviewing his claim for the throne that had once belonged to his father. One of these deities was his mother, Isis, who over the years had protected her son from Seth and patiently watched the boy grow into a handsome, adult god.

Standing before the other gods, Horus retold the story of how Seth had cruelly slain Osiris and unjustly usurped the kingship. Then, having made his case, Horus demanded that he be allowed to take his rightful place on the throne. All the gods were impressed by his powers of oratory. And many immediately accepted his claim, agreeing that it would be only right for a king's son to inherit his titles and property. "Indeed," the wise Thoth exclaimed, "Horus's claim to the throne is so right that he could make that claim a million times and it would be just as right each and every time!" Isis was so overjoyed at hearing this pronouncement that she began instructing the north wind to carry the good news straight to Osiris in the Underworld.

Suddenly, a hush fell over the meeting. Ra, the sun god, and Seth, who alone among the gods did not approve of Horus's claim to the throne, stood up to speak. "I feel pity for poor Horus," said Ra. "It is a shame he lost his father and the kingship. But when I look at the two claimants for the throne, I see that Seth is clearly the stronger of the two, and I believe that the strongest should be king." Everyone present was greatly surprised at Ra's remarks. They were not nearly as surprised, however, when Seth delivered this dare: "If Horus wants to challenge me, let him fight me before the assembled gods. I will easily destroy this puny upstart!"

## The Judgment of Neith

"Now, wait just a moment," Thoth objected. "I say that Seth's claim is not legal, since Osiris's rightful heir, Horus, lives and is making his valid claim before us at this very moment." But Thoth's wisdom could not sway Ra from his support for Seth, and the disagreement created an impasse that lasted a full eighty years. Finally the gods agreed to have Thoth, who was the divine scribe, write a letter to the old mother-goddess Neith, to ask for her opinion. It was not long before Neith's answer arrived: "To allow Seth to keep the throne would be an offense against justice," Neith wrote. "You must give Horus what is rightfully his, or else the sky will come crashing down!" But though she sided with Horus, Neith felt it would not be quite fair to leave Seth with nothing. "Give two of Ra's daughters, Anat and Astarte, to Seth as his wives," she advised. "That should help to compensate him for his loss."

Just about everyone thought Neith's suggestions were fair. But once again, Ra dissented. Thinking he had every right, as the chief god, to throw his weight around, the disgruntled sun god began insulting Horus to his face. "You are nothing but a pathetic little weakling," Ra bellowed. "How can you have the audacity to claim the throne of a great land like Egypt?" These insulting remarks made the other gods furious. And the baboon-headed god, Baba, spoke for everyone when he stood up to Ra and said, "Your shrine is empty!"

Ra was shocked because he knew what Baba's words meant—namely that no one took him, the great sun-god, seriously anymore. Suddenly, like a little boy who sulks when he cannot get his way, Ra retreated into his tent and refused to come out or even to speak to anyone. This, in turn, made the other gods feel uneasy, for they worried that Ra might stop sailing his boat of light across the skies, and that would undoubtedly upset nature's balance.

## Seth's Threats, Isis's Trickery

Luckily, another of Ra's daughters, Hathor, thought of a way to brighten her father's mood. She began dancing and singing and stripping off her clothes. To act this way at such a serious moment appeared so silly that it made everyone laugh and applaud. Ra heard the commotion, peeked outside his tent to see what was going on, and could not help but laugh himself. His good mood restored, he called for Horus and Seth to step forward and make their respective cases for the kingship once again.

This time, however, the dispute became increasingly heated. First, Seth claimed that he was the logical choice because, as Ra had said before, he, Seth, was the strongest. Seth said: "Each day when Ra sails his boat below the horizon, he travels through the Underworld. Sometimes the evil snake-god, Apophis, attacks the boat and tries to kill Ra. Only I, protector of the gods, with my mighty scepter, can save him."

Many of the gods had to admit that Seth had a point. However, Thoth continued to argue that it would be more lawful to award the throne to Horus. In addition, Isis made an impassioned speech on behalf of her son that seemed to make most of the gods sympathize with Horus. Livid with rage, Seth roared, "You sniveling cowards! I will teach you the hard way who is the strongest god of all! If you refuse to give in to my demands, I will use my scepter to beat one of you to death each day until you do! Furthermore, I will never recognize the decision of any court of which Isis is a part."

"Very well," said Ra. "We will move our proceedings and continue deliberating the matter on one of the Nile islands. And I will order Nemty, the ferryman, not to allow any woman who resembles Isis to cross over to the island." Then the gods proceeded to move their court, as Ra had ordered. However, Isis, who had years before managed to find her husband's body hundreds of miles from home, was too clever to be deterred by this action. With ease, she disguised herself as an old woman and offered Nemty, the ferryman, a gold ring if he would but row her across. Completely fooled, he did as she asked.

Once on the Nile island, Isis changed her appearance again, this time into a beautiful young woman. When she saw Seth approaching, she pretended to cry. "What is wrong, my pretty young thing?" Seth inquired. "Can I possibly help you?"

"I hope so," she answered. "My husband, a herdsman, recently died, and my son, as is the law and custom, took charge of his cattle. But then an arrogant stranger came, kicked my son out, and claimed our cattle for himself."

"The scoundrel!" said Seth indignantly. "Fear not, my dear. I will see that this man is punished and that your son regains his rightful inheritance."

"Ha ha, just as I thought!" Isis screamed, as she turned herself into a kite and flew to the top of a nearby tree. "You have just condemned yourself, Seth, for the case I cited was completely identical to the one you are disputing with my son, Horus!"

Seth's blunder cost him greatly. The gods, who had been watching the exchange, finally decided in Horus's favor, and soon the son of Osiris felt the white crown of Egypt being placed on his head.

## Osiris Intervenes

Still, Seth would not accept the verdict of the divine court. "If you are truly worthy of the kingship," he told Horus, "you must be able to meet and overcome all challengers. Therefore, I challenge you to meet me in mortal combat. And the winner shall be Egypt's king!"

Eager to prove himself, Horus accepted his uncle's dare, and a series of fantastic and dangerous battles ensued. In the first, the two gods transformed themselves into huge hippopotamuses and plunged into the deep river, where their battle sent great waves crashing over the riverbanks. Attempting to aid her son, Isis quickly fashioned a copper harpoon and, hoping to kill Seth with it, sent it hurtling into the water. Unfortunately, however, it hit Horus instead! After using her magic powers to remove the harpoon from her son, Isis threw it again, and this time she managed to spear Seth.

"For pity's sake," wailed Seth, as he surfaced, bleeding, "I am your brother! Surely you wouldn't kill your own brother, would you?" Isis thought this was a strange thing for Seth to say, considering that earlier he had killed his own brother, Osiris. Yet she took pity on Seth anyway and pulled the harpoon out. Her sparing of Seth angered Horus so much that he lost his temper, cut off his mother's head, and strode off into the mountains. The other gods were horrified by this act, and Ra vowed that Horus would be punished. First, they restored Isis to her familiar form, and then they went looking for Horus.

As it turned out, Seth was the first to find Horus, who lay sleeping under a tree. Wasting no time, Seth jumped on his nephew, gouged out his eyes, and buried them in the desert. Once more, a sympathetic goddess intervened on Horus's behalf. This time it was the lovely sky-goddess Hathor, who rubbed his empty eye sockets with milk from a gazelle, which made his eyes grow back. With Horus restored to his old self, it was not long before he and Seth were at each other's throats again.

Finally, after many more contests and fights, Osiris, lord of the Underworld, settled the dispute once and for all. In a letter to the divine court, he said, "You should not have denied my son his rightful inheritance, and you must give it to him immediately. Do not be foolish enough to defy my will; for there are terrible serpents and other creatures I can let loose to ravage the earth's surface; moreover, consider that even you, the gods, must eventually sink below the horizon into my realm, where you will then be under my power and susceptible to my wrath."

These threats made all the gods, including the mighty Ra, think twice. So they restored Horus as king of Egypt. And even after his reign had ended, he remained on the throne, in a very real sense, forever, as a force inhabiting every living pharaoh. As for Seth, Ra took him into the sky. Ever since, Seth's voice has been frequently heard in the form of thunder.

# QUESTIONS AND ANSWERS

**Q:** *What did Horus demand of the gods who sat in judgment?*

**A:** He demanded that he be given what he believed was rightfully his—the throne of Egypt, which had once belonged to his father, Osiris.

**Q:** *What dare did Seth deliver to Horus in front of the other gods?*

**A:** Seth dared Horus to fight him for possession of the throne of Egypt.

**Q:** *When Baba, the baboon-headed god, told Ra, the sun god, that his shrine was "empty," what did he mean?*

**A:** The image of an empty shrine symbolized a ruler whose subjects no longer took him seriously.

**Q:** *Why did Ra's reaction make the other gods uneasy?*

**A:** Ra's hurt and angry mood made the other gods worry that he might suddenly refuse to sail his boat of light across the sky. In that case, the normal cycle of day and night would be upset, perhaps with disastrous results.

**Q:** *How did Isis trick Seth into condemning himself?*

**A:** Isis, disguised as a young woman, told Seth a story about having a son who had been cheated out of his rightful inheritance. The situation in the story was similar to the one in which Seth was trying to deny Horus his right to sit on Egypt's throne. By offering to help the distressed woman's son regain his inheritance, Seth unconsciously revealed that he understood his own actions against Horus were immoral and wrong.

**Q:** *In the first battle between Seth and Horus, what form did the two gods assume?*

**A:** Seth and Horus became hippopotamuses and fought in the Nile River.

**Q:** *Who finally intervened and put an end to the rivalry and bickering between Horus and Seth?*

**A:** Osiris, Horus's father and lord of the Underworld, intervened. Osiris threatened to unleash terrifying serpents and other monsters onto the earth and punish the gods when they reached the Underworld if the gods did not place Horus on the throne.

# EXPERT COMMENTARY

The goddesses Anat and Astarte, who end up as Ra's daughters (and gifts for Seth) in Horus's myth, began as Middle Eastern, rather than Egyptian, deities. According to University of London scholar George Hart:

> These Middle Eastern goddesses had become incorporated in the Egyptian pantheon [group of gods] in the New Kingdom [around 1150–1070 B.C.], as had the important Syrian gods Baal and Reshep. Since Seth has an affinity [is identified] with foreign warrior gods, the gift of these two goddesses is quite apt.[3]

Because Horus was a sky god, the Egyptians often interpreted his eyes as the sun and moon. At one point in the myth in which he battles with Seth, Horus loses his eyes. Noted Egyptologists Ian Shaw and Paul Nicholson explain how one of Horus's eyes came to have special significance as a symbol:

> During his contendings [disputes] with Seth, Horus is said to have lost his left eye (which represented the moon), although fortunately the goddess Hathor was able to restore it. The *udjat-* or *wedjat*-eye (the "eye of Horus") therefore came to symbolize the general process of "making whole" and healing, the term *udjat* literally meaning "sound." It also represented the waxing [getting larger] and waning [getting smaller] of the moon, and served as a metaphor [descriptive figure of speech] for protection, strength, and perfection; *wedjat*-eye amulets [objects worn around the neck to ward off evil] are extremely common [tokens used in ancient Egypt].[4]

# 5

# The Near Destruction of Humanity

## INTRODUCTION

The ancient Egyptians believed that as long as humans maintained the proper relationship with the gods, these deities would look on them favorably, and life on earth would continue and prosper. Maintaining a proper relationship with the gods involved a number of factors. Most importantly, priests in temples throughout Egypt were expected to perform certain daily rituals and to offer up sacrifices (of plants, animals, and food and drink) to the gods; and people, from the loftiest monarchs to the lowliest peasants, were expected never to offend the gods in any way. So long as the human race met these conditions, it could expect to keep the gods on its side.

If, on the other hand, the gods perceived that humanity was not fulfilling its duty to the relationship, divine punishment was certain to follow. The so-called "Myth of Cataclysm" (catastrophe or disaster) was widely viewed as a warning to humans of what destructive powers the gods were capable of if provoked or angered. The myth comes from a collection of magical spells called the *Book of the Divine Cow*. Sections of this work were discovered in the tombs of the pharaohs Tutankhamun, who is known today simply as "King Tut" (reigned 1333–1323 B.C.), and Sety I (reigned 1294–1279 B.C.), as well as in other royal tombs.[1]

Today, King Tut is perhaps the most famous of ancient Egypt's rulers, with the possible exception of Cleopatra. This is because of the tremendous amount of publicity that was generated when archaeologists discovered his tomb in 1922. What made the find so special was that the tomb was almost intact, with only a minimal amount of damage and thievery inflicted by grave robbers, who over the years ransacked and ruined most other Egyptian royal burial sites. Among Tut's treasures were his magnificent throne, made of gold and decorated with gems, and his golden sarcophagus, or coffin, which held his remains.

The Myth of Cataclysm is set in the dim past, when the sun god Ra was still Egypt's ruler. Besides Ra, the myth includes his daughter Hathor, who was often referred to as the Eye of Ra. Usually seen as the sun's disk, the Eye of Ra could also be a separate entity that Ra sent out to perform a task, and it sometimes took the form of his daughter, Hathor. Other characters in the myth include: Nu, the primeval ocean and one of the Ogdoad of Hermopolis; Nut, mother of Osiris and Isis; Thoth, god of wisdom and writing; and a human—the high priest of Heliopolis.

## THE NEAR DESTRUCTION OF HUMANITY

### The Wisdom of Nu

The mighty Ra had ruled the land of Egypt for so long that no human being could conceive of, let alone count, the number of years. Although the sun god had governed fairly and well, it was clear that he was becoming old and frail, for apparently even the deathless ones were somewhat susceptible to the aging process when they took an earthly form. Consequently, various groups of people in different parts of Egypt began to question Ra's continued ability to rule. They held secret meetings behind his back, and some began plotting to overthrow him and set a human king on his throne.

What these conspirators did not realize was that Ra, frail or not, still held many important powers. Among them were extremely acute senses of sight and hearing; thus he was able to watch and overhear the plotters as they drew their plans against him. Ra decided that something had to be done to teach these ungrateful humans a lesson, so he secretly convened a council made up of most of the gods to ask for their advice.

"Why have you asked us to come here?" they inquired. Ra proceeded to tell them of the humans' treachery. Then he turned to Nu, the oldest among the council members, the dark abyss from whom he himself had originally risen. Nu's great age, Ra reasoned, could surely be expected to produce considerable wisdom.

"From the tears of my own eyes I gave these mortal creatures life," said Ra. "And now, see how they repay me by plotting to do away with me and rule Egypt, by themselves, without Ra as their leader. Tell me, great Nu, what punishment should I unleash on them?"

"You have every right to feel betrayed and angry, my son," replied Nu without hesitation. "You are indeed a great god—even greater than I, who gave you life. And the humans should not be allowed to escape your punishment. In my opinion, that punishment should take the form of your divine and fearful Eye. Send the Eye of Ra to chastise these thankless ones!"

Hearing this pronouncement, the rest of the gods sang out almost in unison, "Nu speaks wisely. Send the Eye of Ra to strike down these guilty ones, these transgressors against divine justice! Kill them all!"

## Hathor's Bloody Rampage

"I shall do as you suggest, my fellow divinities," Ra agreed, nodding his head. Looking out upon the land, he saw many of the humans scurrying about, leaving their homes and cities, and fleeing into the desert. It was clear that somehow the conspirators had learned of the meeting of the gods and now hoped they could hide from Ra's wrath by running away. But they were sorely mistaken. For at this moment the Eye of Ra appeared in the form of the goddess Hathor. Often the humans had seen her as a kind and loving deity, a sort of generous mother-figure; but now they were about to discover her darker side. When she stood before her father as the instrument of his vengeance, no words passed between them, for none were needed.

Hathor whirled in a fury. She leaped into the sky and flew out over the desert, where she easily found the conspirators against her father cowering behind rocks and inside crevices. Transforming herself into a gigantic and vicious lioness, she swooped down on them, rending and tearing their bodies, as the others scattered in terror. One by one, in groups, and indeed by the thousands, she slaughtered them and drank their blood, which splattered over her and soaked the sands. When she had killed all who had hidden in the desert, she began attacking the villages and cities, smashing down houses and devouring every human being she could find. Even innocent children and infants were not safe from her rampage.

All day long, Ra sat quietly, watching his daughter Hathor's murderous spree. The prayers, as well as the screams, of the dying reached his ears, and his mood steadily changed. "There is no doubt that the human conspirators deserved punishment," he said to himself. "But these men are now all dead. And it seems cruel and wasteful to allow the rest of humanity to suffer for the crimes of a handful of men." Ra also reasoned that if all the humans were killed, he and the other gods would have no one left to worship them.

## The Lady of Drunkenness

Therefore, when darkness came and Hathor rested from her attacks, Ra urged her to quench her rage. "You have fulfilled my wish to punish the humans," he said. "There is no need to kill any more of them." But his daughter was in no mood for such meek and sympathetic talk. The taste of human blood had excited her, and she was anxious to resume her killing spree in the morning, when she planned to finish the grisly job she had started. "You cannot change my mind," she told Ra. Then she lay down and went to sleep.

Seeing that Hathor was out of control, Ra decided that he would have to resort to trickery to keep her from killing the rest of humanity. Quickly, he summoned the swiftest messengers he could find and ordered them to run as fast as a shadow to the site of Aswan, a city far to the south, where the soil was very red. The messengers' task was to bring back as much of this red ocher as possible before morning dawned.

Meanwhile, Ra enlisted the aid of his high priest at Heliopolis and the priest's slave girls. When the messengers returned with several large baskets of ocher, the high priest hurriedly made a red dye from the colored earth; and as swiftly as they could, the slave girls brewed seven thousand jars of beer. Not long before sunup, at Ra's orders, the high priest mixed the red dye into the beer, producing a mixture that looked almost exactly like blood. Very carefully, so as not to awaken Hathor, Ra poured out the red-colored beer, forming a huge puddle on the ground near where she slept.

No sooner had Ra finished when morning broke and Hathor awakened, ready and eager to resume her slaughter.

"What is this?" she exclaimed, suddenly spying the large red puddle. "More human blood!" she chortled, and immediately began lapping it up. Just as Ra had hoped, drinking so much beer so quickly made his daughter extremely intoxicated. Soon she felt woozy, tired, and could no longer remember why her father had sent her into Egypt. Dragging her feet, the drunken goddess went back to sleep and did not wake up for many days. This was why, in later ages, Hathor became known as the "lady of drunkenness" and people drank strong beer when celebrating at her festivals.

## The Ascension of Ra

The whole episode had several lessons to teach. The surviving humans learned that they must not insult or plot against the immortal gods. Hathor learned to control her lethal temper. And Ra came to the conclusion that he was indeed too old and tired to rule Egypt properly. What is more, the slaughter of so many innocent people had made his heart sad. Now he longed only to rise into the heavens, where thereafter he would sail his boat of light across the sky every day.

Hearing of Ra's wish to leave Egypt and reign in the sky, Nu arrived with the goddess Nut. At Nu's order, Nut transformed herself into what later came to be called the Divine Cow. Seated on the cow's back, Ra, gleaming with a divine radiance, rose proudly into the heavens, while the humans looked on in awe. As a last parting gift to the surviving mortals, the sun god ordered Thoth to watch over them and to teach them the art of writing, the first step toward a higher civilization.

# QUESTIONS AND ANSWERS

**Q:** *What important powers did Ra still command?*

**A:** Ra had acute senses of sight and hearing.

**Q:** *Why did Ra decide to punish the human race?*

**A:** The humans had begun to question the sun god's ability to rule Egypt and had also begun to plot his overthrow.

**Q:** *What instrument did Ra choose to punish the humans? And what form did this instrument take?*

**A:** Ra chose the Eye of Ra. In this case the Eye of Ra took the form of a separate living entity—Ra's daughter, the goddess Hathor. Although the Egyptians often pictured her as a nurturing deity who fed humans milk, at Ra's urging she now morphed into a terrifying instrument of revenge and destruction.

**Q:** *Into what animal did Hathor transform herself to carry out her murderous rampage?*

**A:** She turned herself into a huge and vicious lioness with sharp teeth and claws.

**Q:** *Why did Ra change his mind about punishing the humans?*

**A:** He felt sad and responsible for all the lives being taken, and thought it was unfair for innocent people to pay for the crimes of just a few men. He also reasoned that if all humans were killed, there would be none left to worship the gods.

**Q:** *After Ra changed his mind and decided to spare the surviving humans, how did he manage to stop his bloodthirsty daughter's killing spree?*

***A:*** With the aid of the high priest of Heliopolis, Ra prepared a large batch of beer that had been colored red to look like blood. The sun god poured the beer onto the ground near Hathor, who was sleeping. When she awoke, she thought the beer was blood, drank it, and became intoxicated. Then she went back to sleep, ending her rampage.

**Q:** *What lessons were learned by the characters in this story?*

***A:*** The humans who survived learned to obey the gods and never to plot against them or underestimate their powers. Hathor learned to control her temper. And Ra learned that the time must come even for gods to retire.

**Q:** *After he was finished ruling Egypt, what became Ra's principal role in the heavens?*

***A:*** His job was to sail a boat of light across the sky every day, providing the people on earth with light and warmth.

# EXPERT COMMENTARY

In an excerpt from his book about Egyptian myths, the late scholar Lewis Spence provides valuable information about the mysterious, many-faceted goddess Hathor, who, according to the Myth of Cataclysm, nearly destroyed humanity:

> It is no easy matter to gauge the true mythological significance of the Egyptian goddess Hathor, patron of women, of love, and of pleasure . . . . We find a multitude of mythological ideas fused in the Hathor conception: She is a moon-goddess, a sky-goddess, a goddess of the east, a goddess of the west . . . an agricultural goddess, a goddess of moisture, even on occasion a solar [sun] deity. . . . The original form under which Hathor was worshiped was that of a cow. Later she is represented as a woman with the head of a cow, and finally with a human head, the face broad, kindly, placid, and decidedly bovine [cow-like], sometimes retaining the ears or horns of the animal she represents.[2]

In a sort of sequel to the story of Hathor's rampage against humankind, Ra directs Thoth to teach the survivors how to write. The modern mythologist Veronica Ions describes why Thoth was the natural choice for this task:

> Another role of Thoth [besides those of dispenser of wisdom and master magician] . . . was that of Master of the Words of God, or of the characters of writing, which he was universally said to have invented. The connection with magic is clear, for the texts were the clue to all religious mysteries. Thoth himself was supposed to have written with his own hand a book of magic and the forty-two volumes which contained all the wisdom of the world. . . . As a scribe and secretary of Ra, he was worshiped by scribes and all the learned men in Egypt, including of course the priests.[3]

# 6

# The Princess and the Demon

## INTRODUCTION

Some Egyptian myths concerned real people, usually pharaohs or other royal personages, who had made important names for themselves in ages long past. This was the case with the tale most often referred to as "The Princess and the Demon." In the third century B.C., when a Greek dynasty, the Ptolemies, ruled Egypt, some priests inscribed the story on a stele that now rests in the famous Louvre Museum in Paris.[1]

For reasons unknown, in recording their version of the myth, the priests chose the time and setting of a thousand years before, at the royal court of the pharaoh Rameses II, one of Egypt's most famous and accomplished rulers. He has traditionally been viewed as the pharaoh against whom the Hebrews, led by Moses, rebelled when they left Egypt for the "promised land"; so Rameses is the pharaoh portrayed in both the silent and sound film versions of *The Ten Commandments*. (This identification is based on some lines in the Old Testament saying that the Hebrew slaves helped build one of Rameses' "treasure cities." However, many scholars remain unsure of whether the Hebrew exodus was a real event, and if it was real, whether it occurred during Rameses' reign.)[2]

In fashioning the tale of The Princess and the Demon, the Ptolemaic priests considerably twisted the facts of Rameses' reign to suit their own purposes. In reality, in 1285 B.C., Rameses fought a huge but indecisive battle against the Hittites, a people inhabiting Asia Minor (now Turkey). Several years later, the two states signed a peace treaty; and they sealed it with a marriage between Rameses and the Hittite king's daughter. In the priests' version of the story inscribed on the stele, by contrast, Rameses marries the daughter of the king of the distant land of Bakhtan (which may either represent ancient Bactria, what is now northern Afghanistan, or else is an imaginary country).

The priests also inserted into the story Khonsu (or Khensu), a moon god sometimes identified with the god Thoth and thought to possess healing powers, particularly the ability to drive away evil spirits inhabiting someone's body. E.A. Wallis Budge, an expert on ancient Egyptian lore, describes how Egyptian priests depicted the god Khonsu in art:

> Whether standing or seated on a throne, he has usually the body of a man with the head of a hawk; sometimes, however, his head also is that of a man. He wears on his head the lunar disk in a crescent, or the solar disk with a uraeus [royal image of a cobra], or the solar disk with the plumes and a uraeus. . . . [Sometimes] he is seen seated on a throne. . . [while other times] he appears. . . in the form of a mummied man seated on a throne; over his forehead is the uraeus of royalty and by the side of his head is the lock of youth.[3]

In addition to Rameses, the king of Bakhtan, and Khonsu, the myth features Rameses' new Bakhtanian bride, whose Egyptian name is Maat-nefru-Ra; his royal scribe, Djeheuty-em-hab; and Maat-nefru-Ra's sister, Princess Bentresh.

# THE PRINCESS AND THE DEMON

## The Royal Sisters from Bakhtan

One day the mighty pharaoh Rameses II decided to leave Egypt to travel to Syria, a region bordering the eastern Mediterranean Sea, several hundred miles north of Egypt. There, he collected tribute, or payment acknowledging submission—in the form of gold and other valuables—from the princes of several surrounding lands. Some of these lands he had recently conquered, while others saw the wisdom of submitting to the pharaoh before he sent his armies against them. Either way, a payment signified that a realm acknowledged Rameses' dominion and authority.

One of these princes, the king of faraway Bakhtan, sent the usual collection of precious metals, rare gems, cartloads of timber, and other valuable commodities. However, Bakhtan also included a very special gift, namely his lovely eldest daughter. He hoped that if Rameses was pleased with her, the pharaoh would allow her to join his harem of Egyptian wives. (By custom, Egyptian kings usually took many wives, forming a group called a harem.) Indeed, the great king of Egypt was much pleased with the girl, for she was not only beautiful, but also intelligent, kind, and generous. In addition, she possessed many talents, including a lovely singing voice and the ability to play the harp and other musical instruments. Captivated with the princess, Ramses gave her an Egyptian name, Maat-nefru-Ra, and soon made her his number-one wife, so that she bore the title of Queen of Egypt.

About a year later, in the summer, Rameses and his court were celebrating the joyous Beautiful Festival of the Valley, honoring the sun god, Ra. At the height of the festivities, a messenger arrived from Bakhtan with news that immediately dampened everyone's pleasant spirits. "Your sister, Princess Bentresh, is gravely ill with a burning fever," the messenger told

Queen Maat-nefru-Ra. Turning to King Rameses, who was obviously quite concerned, the messenger bowed low to show his respect, and then said: "Oh great king, all of the doctors in my land have failed in their attempts to help the princess. Egypt is known far and wide for its skilled doctors and healers. My master, the king of Bakhtan, requests that the great pharaoh, lord of all the lands that lie under the dome of the sky, send a powerful healer to Bakhtan to cure his ailing daughter."

"Of course," Rameses declared without hesitation. "I will do everything I can to help my dear wife's sister. This very day I shall call together all of my best physicians and magicians to decide what should be done."

## Possessed by Evil

True to his word, Rameses consulted with his medical advisors. And all agreed that the palace's chief scribe, Djeheuty-em-hab, who was also a skilled healer, should journey to Bakhtan to diagnose and hopefully to cure Bentresh's illness. Because that land lay so far from Egypt, Djeheuty-em-hab realized that there was no time to waste. Riding a camel, he traveled as quickly as was humanly possible, often pushing himself day and night and sleeping only when he could no longer keep his eyes open. He crossed seemingly countless rugged mountain ranges, sweltering deserts, deep forests, and wide rivers, until finally, after several difficult months, he reached Bakhtan. There he met briefly with the king, who was greatly relieved and thankful to see him. Then the scribe hurried to Bentresh's bedside. It was obvious that she was still quite ill with a raging fever. Her skin was flushed and hot, her breathing heavy and labored, and she did not seem to recognize her own father, nor anyone else who visited her.

Once Djeheuty-em-hab examined the girl, it became clear to him that the fever was caused by an evil demon that had taken possession of her body. The royal scribe did his best to drive the loathsome spirit out, but his magic was not strong enough. "I'm sorry," he told the king. "But only a god's power can drive away this demon. Your best chance of saving the girl is to ask my master to send one of our Egyptian gods to try."

The king agreed and immediately sent his swiftest messenger to Rameses with the request. Rameses hurried to the temple of the moon god Khonsu in the royal city of Thebes and approached the golden statue of the god, which rested on a magnificent carved pedestal. "Great Khonsu," he said, "who at Hermopolis is called Great Khonsu-Thoth, I come to you today on behalf of my chief wife's sister, the Princess Bentresh. She is under the control of a demon, and my priests tell me that one of the forms you have been known to take is that of demon-expeller. Would it be possible for that manifestation of your divine and righteous self to travel to faraway Bakhtan and heal the girl?" After a few seconds, the great golden statue slowly nodded its head, indicating that the god had agreed to the request.

## Khonsu Fights the Demon

Delighted, Rameses ordered that the statue of Khonsu be carried with great haste, but also with great care, to Bakhtan. A large escort of soldiers, priests, and attendants went along to ensure that the journey remain smooth and trouble-free and that no bandits or other hostile persons damage the sacred statue and thereby anger the god. The travelers crossed the same daunting array of mountains, deserts, forests, and rivers that Djeheuty-em-hab had; the journey was long and tiring, but luckily they encountered no problems.

Reaching their destination, the Egyptian priests transported the divine image into the local palace and then, guided by the king, to Bentresh's bedside. Almost immediately, there was a deep rumbling noise, and the sacred statue began to glow. The king, priests, and others in the room were filled with awe and bowed low, as Khonsu the demon-expeller suddenly materialized before them. Floating in a brilliantly radiant sphere, the hawk-headed god bent over the feverish girl and placed his hands on her burning forehead. Then both he and the princess began to shake, for Khonsu and the demon were now engaged in a fierce battle.

It did not take long for Khonsu to win the battle, for no evil spirit could withstand his powerful magic for long. The demon, a hideous, twisted-looking creature with leathery skin and yellow eyes, suddenly exited the girl's body and bowed low before Khonsu. "I admit that I am no match for you, mighty Khonsu," it said. "I pray that you will have mercy and not destroy me completely!"

"So long as you refrain from bothering anyone else in this land, I will spare you," Khonsu replied, for he was indeed a merciful god.

"So be it," sputtered the demon with an audible sigh of relief. "I shall leave Bakhtan forever; all I ask is that its king first grant a feast for you and myself." Khonsu and the king agreed to the demon's request. Then the god and the demon banqueted together, and the demon kept its word and departed in a puff of smoke.

Princess Bentresh then awakened, and it was plain to see that she was completely healed. Her father was overjoyed, but he worried that the demon might return, and decided to keep the statue of Khonsu in Bakhtan. However, after three years the king had a dream in which he saw the god Khonsu, in the form of a golden hawk, rise up from the statue and fly away toward Egypt. Finally realizing that he no right to keep Khonsu from his native land, the king sent the statue back to Rameses, along with a new batch of tribute and his undying gratitude for saving his daughter.

# QUESTIONS AND ANSWERS

**Q:** *Why the did the king of Bakhtan send his daughter to the pharaoh Rameses?*

**A:** She was part of the tribute her father paid to Rameses to ensure that Egypt would not invade and conquer Bakhtan.

**Q:** *Why did Rameses become captivated by the king of Bakhtan's daughter?*

**A:** She was beautiful, intelligent, kind, and generous. She was also musically talented and had a lovely and melodic singing voice.

**Q:** *Who did Rameses send first to try and heal Princess Bentresh?*

**A:** The pharaoh sent his chief scribe, Djeheuty-em-hab, also a skilled healer, to try to help Princess Bentresh.

**Q:** *What illness was Princess Bentresh found to be suffering from?*

**A:** Djeheuty-em-hab determined that she had a fever caused by a demon inhabiting her body.

**Q:** *Why did Rameses send the statue of the god Khonsu to Bakhtan?*

**A:** It was determined that only the powers of an Egyptian god could drive the demon out of the princess. Rameses called upon the god Khonsu to perform the task because he was renowned as a demon-expeller.

**Q:** *After driving the demon out of the princess's body, why did the god Khonsu sit down to a feast with the loathsome creature?*

**A:** Khonsu and the king of Bakhtan made a deal with the demon, who agreed to leave the region forever in return for a banquet. In ancient Egypt, gods and kings, as well as ordinary people, were expected to keep up their end of a bargain, even if the person (or creature) with whom they bargained was repulsive or mean.

**Q:** *What form did Khonsu take in the king's dream, and what did the dream mean?*

**A:** In the dream, Khonsu took the form of a golden hawk that rose up from the statue and flew back to Egypt. The king realized that what he had seen in the dream symbolized the god's need and desire to return to his native land. Therefore, the king, who was grateful to Khonsu for helping his daughter, sent the god's statue back to its home in Egypt.

# EXPERT COMMENTARY

As the story of The Princess and the Demon illustrates, the moon god Khonsu was sometimes linked or identified with Thoth, the god of wisdom and writing. As a moon-god, Khonsu supposedly traveled across the dome of the heavens. Thoth was also revered as a moon deity, as well as a divine messenger-traveler. So it was only natural that priests in some Egyptian regions fused together the identities of the two gods. Scholar Philippe Derchain adds:

> Every time two divinities combine into one and . . . a god has a double name . . . one of the names designates the person . . . while the other designates the function that this person fulfills at a given time. . . . The name of Khonsu-Thoth, for example, simply emphasizes the idea that the moon god Khonsu is capable of maintaining the [moon] on the proper path [by, in a sense, playing the role of Thoth].[4]

Professor Budge adds this further physical description of the god Khonsu as depicted in Egyptian art:

> As "Khonsu, the mighty, who cometh forth from Nu," he is provided with two hawks' heads, one facing to the right and the other to the left, and four wings, and he stands with each foot upon the head of a crocodile; on his heads rest the lunar crescent and disk. In this form he represents both the sun at sunrise and the new moon, and the two crocodiles symbolize the two great powers of darkness over which he has triumphed.[5]

# 7

# The Cleverest Egyptian of Them All

## INTRODUCTION

Although most Egyptian myths derive from stone inscriptions, paintings, papyri, and other surviving Egyptian sources, a few have been preserved only in the writings of neighboring peoples, most often the Greeks. One of the most famous and charming Egyptian myths, about a clever thief who outwitted a great pharaoh, is one of these.

The story's source is the renowned history composed by the fifth-century B.C. Greek writer Herodotus, who later became known as the "father of history." He earned this nickname because so far as we know, he was the first scholar to write a conventional chronicle of real historical events. Previous writers had turned out only works about geography or compilations of legendary figures and events.[1] Herodotus's history is a detailed account of the early fifth-century B.C. invasions of Greece by the Persians (whose empire was located in the area now occupied by Iran and Iraq). But it includes many details about various peoples and places that Herodotus visited in his lengthy and frequent travels.

One of the places Herodotus visited was Egypt, which fascinated him. There, priests and others told him a number of popular tales, some of them involving the gods, and others about famous rulers of past ages. One of these rulers, they said, was Rhampsinitus, the pharaoh who was best known for being bested by a clever thief. In reality, there never was an Egyptian pharaoh by that name; but modern scholars think he may have been a confused memory of Rameses III, who ruled from 1184 to 1153 B.C.[2] As for whether any of the incidents in the myth actually happened, no one can say

## THE CLEVEREST EGYPTIAN OF THEM ALL

### The New Treasure Room

In all of Egypt's history, so it is said, no pharaoh was wealthier than Rhampsinitus, who possessed gold, silver, precious gems, and other treasures in incredible abundance. Not surprisingly, he worried that someone might try to steal his treasures. That would make him a poor king, and in Rhampsinitus's mind a poor king was a powerless one who would not be remembered by his people after he had passed on to Osiris's nether realm beneath the horizon.

Consequently, Rhampsinitus ordered that a special treasure room be built along one side of the palace. "There are to be no windows and only a single door," he told the architect. "Furthermore, I want you to construct the walls, floor, and ceiling out of huge stone blocks that a man with a large ax would not be able to chip away, even if he worked at it day and night for twenty years." The architect carried out the king's instructions and built the new, seemingly indestructible and robbery-proof treasure room. Then Rhampsinitus had all of his treasure placed inside and stationed his most trusted guards at the door, confident that no thief could ever gain entrance.

However, what the king did not count on was that the architect, in addition to being an expert builder, was a very clever man. While constructing the room, the architect cut into two pieces one of the stone blocks destined for the back, outer wall. One of the two pieces he cemented in place; but the other, which was light enough for one man to move with some considerable effort, he left loose. He inserted it so perfectly into the wall that the seam was practically invisible to the eye.

## The Architect's Two Sons

Several years passed and the architect, who was growing old, fell gravely ill. Lying on his deathbed, he summoned his two young sons and whispered to them the secret of the treasure room and its loose stone. "I do not want you boys to go through life having to bow and scrape for a living," he said, "while that greedy pharaoh of ours hoards more wealth than he deserves. When I am dead and gone, search out the stone, enter the treasure room, and carry away some of his wealth for yourselves. All that I ask is that you take care not to become as greedy as he is."

About a month later, after their father's funeral, the young men waited until it was dark and made their way to the palace wall. There they found the loose stone in the exact spot their father had indicated. Removing the stone and climbing inside the room, the brothers lit a torch and, to their awe and delight, saw the king's magnificent treasures glittering in the yellow-orange glow. Quietly, so as not to alert the guards, they stuffed their pockets with gold coins and some jewelry and exited the room the same way they had entered. Then they replaced the stone.

The next day, King Rhampsinitus went to the treasure room to get a prized necklace for one of his wives. He saw that the guards were still on duty, and he also checked to make sure the seal he had placed on the door was unbroken. "My treasure must still be safe," he thought reassuringly to himself. But when he entered the room and found the necklace, along with some other jewelry, missing, his confidence began to evaporate. "How can this be?" he muttered. "The guards saw nothing, and the door seal was unbroken."

The king's frustration grew as night after night the same scenario played out. The brothers sneaked into the treasure room, stole whatever they could carry, and escaped; and the next day the king discovered the theft, but could not fathom how it had been accomplished. Finally, the king ordered that a trap, made of heavy metal clamps, be set inside the room.

That very night the brothers entered the treasure room as usual, and it did not take long for one of them to get his legs ensnared in the trap's metal clamps. Try as he might, the other brother was unable to free him. "If they find me in here in the morning, they will come looking for you and our whole family will be punished," said the trapped brother. "There is only one thing to be done. You must cut off my head and take it with you. That way no one will be able to identify me, and our family will be safe." Sobbing with grief, the second brother, who agreed that there was no alternative, carried out those instructions.

## His Cleverest Deed

The next morning, when Rhampsinitus discovered the headless body in his treasure room, he cried out in anger. Since someone had to have removed the man's head from the room, the king reasoned, there must still be a second thief at large! In an effort to draw the living thief out, Rhampsinitus had the body of the dead one hung from the outside palace wall and placed guards nearby. If anyone attempted to retrieve the body, the guards would arrest him and the thief would be caught at last. At least, this is what the king thought would happen.

Instead, the surviving brother, who was, it turned out, even more clever than his father, devised a brilliant plan. First, he collected several goatskins, filled them with wine, put them on donkeys, and herded the animals past the guards outside the palace wall. Secretly, he cut two of the skins slightly open to allow the wine to begin flowing out. Then he began screaming, "My master will beat me for this!" Seeing what was happening, some of the guards came over to help the young man save the wine; and before long he had become friendly with them and offered them the wine in the remaining goatskins. Once the drunken guards had fallen asleep and night had fallen, he cut down his brother's body and escaped with it.

When the king heard of this trickery, he was more frustrated than ever. "So help me," he swore, "I will outwit this fellow somehow." This time Rhampsinitus devised a plan that involved his daughter, the royal princess. "I will issue a proclamation," he told her, "saying that any man in the kingdom can speak to you and that you will grant him whatever favor he desires. But first, he will have to tell you the cleverest thing he has ever done. When our thief reveals himself in this way, he will be my prisoner at last!"

But once more, the king's plan backfired. Hearing the proclamation and guessing that it was meant to be a trap, the thief went to a cemetery, cut an arm off a corpse, and hid the severed limb under his robe. When it was his turn to meet with the princess, she posed the question about his cleverest deed. Confidently, the thief told her about getting the guards drunk and escaping with his brother's body. When she heard this news, the princess grabbed hold of his arm and called out to the guards. "I have caught the thief!" she yelled triumphantly. But then, to her horror, she noticed that the man was gone and she was left holding the severed arm, which the thief had cleverly made to look like his own.

Having been outwitted so many times, Rhampsinitus decided that it was useless to waste any more energy trying to catch the thief. Admitting defeat, the king issued another proclamation, this time offering the thief a pardon and a rich reward if he would come forward and reveal his identity. A few days later, the architect's son arrived at the palace and presented himself to the king in front of the entire royal court.

"You are indeed a clever man to have been able to outwit me," said Rhampsinitus. "Indeed, you are the cleverest Egyptian of them all! You will not only become my royal advisor, but also my son-in-law, for I will give you my daughter's hand in marriage." In this way, Rhampsinitus showed that he was, if not exceedingly clever, at least wise: for now the cleverest living countryman would be his trusted servant forever.

# QUESTIONS AND ANSWERS

**Q:** *How did the architect manage to build the new treasure room to the pharaoh's satisfaction and still make sure that a thief could later get inside without the pharaoh knowing?*

**A:** The architect took a stone block destined for the back wall of the room. Then he cemented one half of the stone into place and left the other half loose, so that a man could remove it and climb inside the room.

**Q:** *How did the king catch one of the thieves?*

**A:** He left a metal trap in the treasure room.

**Q:** *Once one of the brothers had been caught in the king's trap, why did he insist that his brother behead him?*

**A:** With the head still attached, the king and his men could identify the thief, and the authorities would be able to track down the other members of the thief's family and punish them. However, if the king's men found only a headless corpse, there would be no way for them to identify the body.

**Q:** *How did Rhampsinitus try to trick the living brother into appearing?*

**A:** He had the dead brother's headless body hung from the outside palace wall and guarded. The king hoped that a relative would retrieve the body to give it the proper funeral preparations.

**Q:** *How did the thief manage to retrieve his dead brother's body?*

**A:** He paraded some donkeys laden with wineskins past the guards. Then he offered the guards the remaining wine, got them intoxicated, and ran off with his brother's body.

**Q:** *How did the clever thief escape once the princess began yelling for the guards?*

**A:** Earlier he had gone to a cemetery and cut an arm off a corpse. While he was speaking to the princess, he made it look as though the dead person's arm was his own. When she tried to grab him, she found herself holding only the severed limb.

**Q:** *Why, after all the thief's attempts to rob him, did Rhampsinitus decide to make him the royal advisor?*

**A:** The pharaoh showed his wisdom in appointing the thief to such a high position. Now, the cleverest man in Egypt would be his personal advisor, which meant that the king would receive the best possible advice.

# EXPERT COMMENTARY

In the story, the king's order to hang the beheaded thief's body on the palace wall was unusually harsh by Egyptian standards. And it is not surprising that the surviving thief risked so much to retrieve his brother's remains. The Egyptians had a great deal of respect and religious concern for the dead, so much so that even the remains of executed criminals were normally given to their relatives for proper embalming and burial. Without the benefit of these rites, it was believed, a person could not reach the afterlife. "All men, not just the king . . . hoped that they would enjoy eternal life," scholar Veronica Ions explains, "and . . . the chief hope of survival in the afterlife was to identify completely with the passion [death and resurrection story] of Osiris and to copy the exact forms of his embalmment."[3] Thus, Rhampsinitus's order to deny the body proper burial was widely viewed as cruel, and the surviving thief would likely stop at nothing to make sure his brother reached the afterlife.

In his account of the story of Rhampsinitus and the clever thief, Herodotus presents an unusual amount of detail about one particular episode, namely the one in which the thief tricks the guards by getting them drunk. (Perhaps the historian, or the Egyptian priests who told him the story, felt that the scene was the most vivid illustration of the thief's cleverness.) Here is part of the scene in question, in Herodotus's own words:

> He [the thief] filled some skins with wine and loaded them onto donkeys, which he drove to the place where the soldiers were guarding his brother's corpse. Arrived there, he gave a pull on the necks of two or three of the skins, which undid the fastenings. The wine poured out, and he roared and banged his head, as if not knowing which donkey to deal with first, while the soldiers, seeing the wine streaming all over the road, seized their pots and ran to catch it, congratulating themselves on such a piece of luck. The young man swore at them in pretended rage, which the soldiers did their best to soothe, until finally he changed his tune, and, appearing to have recovered his temper, drove the donkeys out of the roadway and began to rearrange the

wine-skins on their backs. Meanwhile, as he chatted with the soldiers, one of them cracked a joke at his expense and made him laugh, whereupon he made them a present of a wine-skin, and without more ado they all sat down to enjoy themselves, and urged their benefactor to join the party and share the drink.[4]

# 8

# The Shipwrecked Sailor

## INTRODUCTION

The nature of the Egyptian literature from which most of Egypt's ancient myths derive changed markedly over the course of time. The writings of the historical period that modern scholars call the Old Kingdom (roughly 2690–2180 B.C.) consisted mostly of serious-minded official funerary texts, such as the *Pyramid Texts*. These deal primarily with the gods and semidivine pharaohs and were intended to help the rulers reach the afterlife.

By contrast, the literature of the Middle Kingdom (around 2055–1650 B.C.) was dominated by fictional tales intended mainly to entertain. To a great degree, these myths deal with ordinary people, rather than royalty, and contain references to real social situations and problems. For example, "The Tale of the Eloquent Peasant" depicts a poor person asking the authorities for money for damages inflicted on him by a well-to-do individual who had attacked him. And "The Story of Sinuhe" follows the life of an Egyptian court official who, after getting into trouble, runs away to Syria; but he misses his native land and rejoices when, in old age, he is permitted to return.

Many of these fictional tales also incorporate elements of fantasy and high adventure, in the style of the *Odyssey*, the famous Greek epic poem by Homer. That is certainly the case with "The Shipwrecked Sailor," retold here. Also referred to as "The Enchanted Island," it was recorded on a nineteenth-century B.C. papyrus now in the Egyptian collection at the Moscow Museum.[1]

The structure of the myth is a story within a story within a story (sometimes called a frame story). As the narrator tells the tale, one of the characters begins to tell his own story; and in the course of that account, another character recalls his own personal yarn. (Among the later well-known adventure tales that have utilized this same form are Homer's *Odyssey* and the *1001 Arabian Nights*.)

The story's main setting is an imaginary island somewhere in the Red Sea, the long waterway that borders Egypt in the east. There are references to Nubia, an African region lying south of Egypt. The two main characters are an envoy—an official sent on a mission by the government—and one of his assistants.

## THE SHIPWRECKED SAILOR

### The Cheerless Trader

As the hot summer sun beat down, an Egyptian envoy stood at the railing of his ship. It was floating northward along the Nile River in the direction of the Egyptian capital of Thebes on its return voyage from Nubia. One of the envoy's assistants, who was sitting nearby mending a garment, suddenly noticed that his boss seemed cheerless and depressed. "Why so glum, sir?" asked the assistant, approaching the other man. "You look as though you have lost all your friends and your money, too."

"It might just as well be that way," said the envoy. "As you well know, because of my reputation as a successful trader, the pharaoh sent me to Nubia to bring back a load of gold from the rich mines in that land. But the mines were all empty. What am I going to say to him when I reach Thebes with an empty ship?

My reputation will be ruined. And he will have me scrubbing the floors in the House of the Dead, that dreadful, foul-smelling place where they mummify dead bodies. I just know it."

"Oh, come on now, sir," said the assistant, smiling. "Don't despair. Surely the pharaoh will understand that it is not your fault the mines were exhausted. After all, no mine has an endless supply of gold. He cannot expect you to squeeze blood out of a stone, now can he?"

The envoy shook his head and sighed heavily. "I appreciate what you are doing," he said, "but it is no use. Trying to cheer me up is like giving water to a goose that you are going to kill and eat an hour later."

"Ah, but situations that might at first seem hopeless often end up working out much better than you expected," declared the assistant, refusing to give up. "Take, for instance, the very first expedition I ever went on."

## The Shipwreck

The assistant proceeded to tell his boss a fascinating story. And as the tale unfolded, the envoy became increasingly engrossed and seemed to forget his own troubles. "I was just a simple, inexperienced young sailor in those days," the assistant began. "Like this one, the expedition was bound for the Nubian mines, only our boat was bigger because we took the Red Sea route instead of the river. A beauty she was—more than a hundred and eighty feet long and at least a hundred feet wide, I swear it, and with a crew of a hundred and twenty sailors. I got to know some of them quite well, and let me tell you, you have never seen a braver, heartier lot than them.

"As luck would have it, though, their lives were cut short. We were halfway down the coast, sailing along as smooth as silk under a totally cloudless sky, when out of nowhere, or so it seemed, a powerful gale blew up. The courageous crew scurried about, trying desperately to keep the ship on course. But the wind was just too strong, and before we knew it we were out of sight of land. Then a huge wave reared up and smashed into the ship, in a very real sense killing it, for every single man on board died (except for me, of course, since I could not be standing here telling you the story if I died too, now could I?).

"Luckily I was able to grab hold of some floating wreckage, and for a whole day and night I drifted. Finally, I saw an island up ahead, swam for it, and managed to pull myself up onto the beach. I was too exhausted at first to do anything but rest; but by the third day my empty stomach told me it was time to go looking for food. Well, let me tell you, it did not take long to discover that the place was a veritable paradise—with grapes, and figs, and fruits of all kinds, along with plenty of wild birds and fish and other tasty treats. I stuffed myself, I must admit. Can you blame me? Then I lit a fire to make a burnt offering to the gods to thank them for my good fortune."

## The Island's Other Resident

"As near as I can tell," the assistant continued, "the smoke from the fire must have revealed my presence to the island's other resident."

"Do you mean to say that there was another shipwrecked sailor on the island?" asked the envoy, now fascinated by the assistant's narrative.

"Not a sailor, I'm afraid. In fact, not even a human being. All of a sudden a stand of trees shook and parted wide, and through the opening crawled a monstrous snake. It had to be at least fifty feet long and four feet thick, I swear it! But it was not just its size that made it an extraordinary serpent. It had golden scales all along its body, a long beard growing from its chin, and—strangest of all—it could talk! 'Who are you and what are you doing on my island?' the creature demanded. 'If you do not tell me immediately, I'll spit a stream of fire at you and reduce you to a pile of smoldering ashes.'

"Needless to say, I was so terrified that I could not speak, and I am embarrassed to admit that I just fainted dead away. When I woke up, I found myself in the snake's home, a large cave that it had furnished and decorated and made surprisingly comfortable. The snake explained that it had taken pity on me and carefully carried me in its jaws to this place. It promised not to kill me and actually professed that it was relieved at having found a companion, since it was unbearably lonely. It told me that it was not mere chance that had brought me to the island, but rather some kind of divine force. This was an enchanted island, it said, where fruits and vegetables and game existed in abundance at all times and the weather was always pleasant.

"I told the snake that I appreciated its willingness to spare me and that I was relieved at having found so pleasing a spot to be marooned. But marooned I was; and the thought of spending the rest of my life away from my native land filled me with sadness. At this, the snake smiled and told me not to despair. 'Things that might at first seem hopeless often end up working out much better than you expected,' it said."

## A Happy Ending?

"'Take my situation, for example,' the snake continued. 'There were originally seventy-five snakes like me on this island, the others being my relatives and close friends. We frequently played games and enjoyed the fine weather and free, limitless supplies of food. Believe me, you have never seen a heartier, happier lot than we were. But then sudden disaster struck us. A falling star came hurtling out of the heavens and ignited into a great fireball that burned up all of my fond companions. I was the only survivor. Needless to say, I was devastated and even thought of taking my own life. However, in time I came to realize that I still had my health and did not have to worry about making a living or starving, since the enchanted island gave me all I needed. So I managed to overcome my grief. In a similar manner, you will overcome your own apprehensions, for you will be rescued within a few months.'"

"Exactly how the snake was able to foretell the future, I don't know," recalled the assistant. "But its prediction indeed proved accurate. About four months later a ship appeared near the island. On board were some of my friends from back home, who had been searching all over for me. I implored the snake, who had become my close and trusted comrade, to come with me back to civilization. But it said that the island was the only civilization it cared to know. This island was where it was meant to be, and so it must stay, even though its ability to see into the future told it that the island would one day sink beneath the waves and disappear forever. As a parting gift, the snake gave me a precious cargo of spices, rare oils and perfumes, giraffe tails, monkeys, and other exotic valuables. With a touch of sadness, I bade it farewell and departed on the ship.

"When I reached Egypt, I went to the palace and asked to see the king. I told him my wondrous tale and presented him with the gifts the snake had given me. And he was so moved that he made me a palace official. You see? My misfortune of being shipwrecked had an unexpectedly happy ending."

The envoy placed his hands on the assistant's shoulders and grinned broadly. "That was one of the best stories I ever heard, my good man. It was, I must admit, thoroughly entertaining. You certainly managed to take my mind off my troubles for awhile, and I appreciate it. But I am afraid I do not have any cargo of valuables to offer the king, as you say you did."

The envoy then turned away, leaned on the railing, and slipped back into his melancholy mood, for he knew he would soon have to face the pharaoh empty-handed. No one knows what happened to the envoy after the ship docked in Thebes. But everyone who hears his story hopes that Egypt's ruler was understanding and did not punish him for his failure to bring back a ship full of gold.

# QUESTIONS AND ANSWERS

**Q:** *How does the structure of the myth "The Shipwrecked Sailor" help to drive home its theme?*

**A:** The myth is told in the complex form of a frame story, or "story within a story within a story." The person recording the story tells us about the envoy and his assistant on the ship. Within that story, the assistant tells the envoy the story of the shipwreck and enchanted island; and within that story, the snake tells the assistant/sailor the story of how it survived the death of its fellow snakes. In each case, the teller is trying to make the listener take heart, for good things can happen to people when they least expect it; and this message is strengthened by constant repetition.

**Q:** *What is the envoy worried about?*

**A:** The pharaoh sent him to Nubia to bring back a load of gold from the mines there. But the mines were empty, and the envoy was unable to fulfill the pharaoh's request. He is afraid the pharaoh will banish him to the House of the Dead, where bodies are taken to be mummified.

**Q:** *After the assistant has been shipwrecked on the island, he discovers that the place has another resident, a huge talking snake. How did the snake get there?*

**A:** It had always lived on the island, along with over seventy others of its kind.

**Q:** *What happened to the other snakes?*

**A:** A falling star turned into a great explosion of fire that killed all the others.

**Q:** *When a rescue ship finally appears, why does the snake refuse to leave the island with the shipwrecked sailor?*

**A:** The snake feels that it was meant to live out its life on the island and has no desire to travel to a strange place inhabited by an alien culture.

**Q:** *Why does the assistant's story ultimately fail to cheer up the envoy?*

**A:** Although the story has entertained him and momentarily taken his mind off his troubles, the envoy cannot forget that he must soon face the pharaoh empty-handed. And there is no way to know if the pharaoh will be understanding and forgive him for bringing back an empty ship.

# EXPERT COMMENTARY

The plot and characters of the myth of The Shipwrecked Sailor reflect the fact that during the period of the Middle Kingdom, Egyptian traders and travelers became increasingly common. Lewis Spence, a scholar on Egyptian lore, elaborates:

> Some of the most interesting passages in Egyptian literature are those that deal with travel and adventure. The natives of Egypt were by no means travelers, and for the most part confined their journeys and excursions to the precincts of their own country, and even to their own . . .provinces. . . .But it was necessary that ambassadors should be sent to the surrounding states, and that tribute that had been agreed upon should be properly enforced. As the benefits of trade grew apparent, Egyptian merchants pushed their way into the surrounding regions, and criminals often saved themselves by flight into foreign countries. Those who had sojourned [lived for a while] abroad were wont [accustomed] upon return home to gather their friends and neighbors about them and regale [entertain] them with an account of their travels.[2]

In the original papyrus version of the myth, the snake tells the sailor that he has been shipwrecked on the "island of Ka." "This phrase is difficult to translate," says University of London scholar George Hart:

> The "Ka" is the life force of a person born at the same time as the physical body but surviving physical death as a spiritual entity. One Egyptologist has suggested that "phantom island" might be a possible rendering. However, since the "Ka" is a magical power, capable of bringing to reality inanimate representations of, for example, bread, beer jugs, incense, linen clothing, and animals, then "the Enchanted Island" is probably the snake's meaning.[3]

# Glossary

***akhet***—The Egyptian flood season, lasting from June through September.

**amulet**—An object worn around the neck as a charm against evil.

***atef***—Worn by the king of Egypt, a white crown shaped somewhat like a bowling pin with a plume attached to either side.

***ba***—In ancient Egypt, the part of the soul representing the personality.

**cataclysm**—A catastrophe or disaster.

**cosmogony**—A story explaining the origin of the universe, or cosmos, and its contents.

**cosmology**—The study of the nature and structure of the universe, or cosmos.

**crook and flail**—The chief insignia of Egyptian royalty, often held by a pharaoh while sitting on his throne. The crook was a royal scepter shaped like a hook; the flail was a stick with long tassels hanging from one end.

**dynasty**—A line of rulers belonging to a single family.

**inscription**—Words and/or pictures carved into stone.

***ka***—In ancient Egypt, the part of the soul representing a person's life force.

**monotheistic**—Believing in one god.

**mummification**—A process for preserving the human body after death.

**natrum**—A mineral salt used to dry out bodies during mummification.

***nome***—In ancient Egypt, a local district.

**papyrus**—An early kind of paper made from sedge, a plant that thrives in marshes.

***peret***—The Egyptian planting season, lasting from October to February.

**pharaoh**—A king of ancient Egypt.

**polytheistic**—Believing in more than one god.

**pyramid**—A tomb built of brick or stone that housed the remains of royal or noble people.

**scepter**—A staff or baton held by a sovereign or royal person as a symbol of authority.

***shemu***—The Egyptian harvest season, lasting from February to June.

**shroud**—A burial garment, or cloths, wrapped around a corpse.

**stele**—An inscribed stone used as a marker or monument.

**tribute**—Payment, in the form of money or other valuables, made to acknowledge submission to a stronger nation or leader.

**uraeus**—Egypt's royal image of the cobra, a poisonous snake, often seen in painting, sculpture, jewelry, or other artistic renderings.

# Chapter Notes

## Preface

1. H. W. F. Saggs, *Civilization Before Greece and Rome* (New Haven, Conn.: Yale University Press, 1989), p. 24.
2. Charles Freeman, *Egypt, Greece, and Rome* (New York: Oxford University Press, 1996), pp. 33–38.
3. Lionel Casson, *Daily Life in Ancient Egypt* (New York: American Heritage, 1975), p. 11.
4. George Hart, *Egyptian Myths* (Austin: University of Texas Press, 1990), pp. 9–28.
5. Nicolas Grimal, *A History of Egypt* (Cambridge, Mass.: Blackwell, 1992), p. 105.
6. Casson, p. 66.
7. Herodotus, *Histories*, trans. Aubrey de Sélincourt (New York: Penguin Books, 1972), pp.160–161.

## Chapter 1. The Creation of the Gods and Humans

1. Eugene Cruz-Uribe, from personal correspondence of August 18, 1999.
2. Leonard H. Lesko, "Ancient Egyptian Cosmogonies and Cosmology," in Byron E. Shafer, ed., *Religion in Ancient Egypt: Gods, Myths, and Personal Practice* (Ithaca, N.Y.: Cornell University Press, 1991), pp. 90–91.
3. Byron E. Shafer, "Introduction" to Shafer, ed., *Religion in Ancient Egypt: Gods, Myths, and Personal Practice* (Ithaca, N.Y.: Cornell University Press, 1991), pp. 98–101.
4. Ibid., p. 3.
5. George Hart, *Egyptian Myths* (Austin: University of Texas Press, 1990), pp. 26–27.

## Chapter 2. The Murder of Osiris

1. George Hart, *Egyptian Myths* (Austin: University of Texas Press, 1990), pp. 29–33, 39–41, 52–54.
2. Leonard H. Lesko, "Ancient Egyptian Cosmogonies and Cosmology," in Byron E. Shafer, ed., *Religion in Ancient Egypt: Gods, Myths, and Personal Practice* (Ithaca, N.Y.: Cornell University Press, 1991), p. 93.

3. Philippe Derchain, "Death in Egyptian Religion," in Yves Bonnefoy, ed., *Greek and Egyptian Mythologies* (Chicago: University of Chicago Press, 1992), p. 236.
4. Paul Johnson, *The Civilization of Ancient Egypt* (New York: HarperCollins, 1999), pp.127–129.

## Chapter 3. Isis and the Seven Scorpions

1. Richard Patrick, *All Color Book of Egyptian Mythology* (London: Octopus Books, 1972), p. 33.
2. Lionel Casson, *Daily Life in Ancient Egypt* (New York: American Heritage, 1975), pp. 60–65.
3. H. W. F. Saggs, *Civilization Before Greece and Rome* (New Haven, Conn.: Yale University Press, 1989), pp. 240–266.
4. Donald Mackenzie, *Egyptian Myths and Legends* (New York: Gramercy Books, 1994), p. xxxvi.
5. Apuleius, *The Golden Ass*, trans. P.G. Walsh (New York: Oxford University Press, 1995), pp. 220–221.
6. Lionel Casson, *Ancient Egypt* (New York: Time-Life, 1965), p. 163.

## Chapter 4. The Revenge of Horus

1. Lewis Spence, *Ancient Egyptian Myths and Legends* (New York: Dover Publications, 1990), p. 96.
2. George Hart, *Egyptian Myths* (Austin: University of Texas Press, 1990), pp. 29, 37–39.
3. Ibid., p. 34.
4. Ian Shaw and Paul Nicholson, *The Dictionary of Ancient Egypt* (New York: Harry N. Abrams, 1995), pp. 133–134.

## Chapter 5. The Near Destruction of Humanity

1. George Hart, *Egyptian Myths* (Austin: University of Texas Press, 1990), p. 47.
2. Lewis Spence, *Ancient Egyptian Myths and Legends* (New York: Dover Publications, 1990), pp. 162–163.
3. Veronica Ions, *Egyptian Mythology* (New York: Peter Bedrick Books, 1982), p. 85.

## Chapter 6. The Princess and the Demon

1. Charles Freeman, *Egypt, Greece, and Rome* (New York: Oxford University Press, 1996), pp. 272–273, 278.

2. Nicolas Grimal, *A History of Egypt* (Cambridge, Mass.: Blackwell, 1992), pp. 258–259.
3. E.A. Wallis Budge, *The Gods of the Egyptians* vol. 2 (New York: Dover Publications, 1969), p. 36.
4. Philippe Derchain, "The Divine and the Gods in Ancient Egypt," in Yves Bonnefoy, ed., *Greek and Egyptian Mythologies* (Chicago: University of Chicago Press, 1992), p. 228.
5. Budge, p. 37.

## Chapter 7. The Cleverest Egyptian of Them All

1. Michael Grant, *Greek and Roman Historians: Information and Misinformation* (New York: Routledge, 1995), pp. 5–7.
2. Nicolas Grimal, *A History of Egypt* (Cambridge, Mass.: Blackwell, 1992), pp. 270–276.
3. Veronica Ions, *Egyptian Mythology* (New York: Peter Bedrick Books, 1982), p. 130.
4. Herodotus, *Histories*, trans. Aubrey de Sélincourt (New York: Penguin Books, 1972), p. 176.

## Chapter 8. The Shipwrecked Sailor

1. George Hart, *Egyptian Myths* (Austin: University of Texas Press, 1990), pp. 72–74.
2. Lewis Spence, *Ancient Egyptian Myths and Legends* (New York: Dover Publications, 1990), p. 190.
3. Hart, p. 73.

# Further Reading


Allen, J.R. *Genesis in Egypt: The Philosophy of Ancient Egyptian Creation Accounts*. New Haven, Conn.: Yale University Press, 1988.

Apuleius. *The Golden Ass*. Trans. P. G. Walsh. New York: Oxford University Press, 1995.

Bonnefoy, Yves, ed. *Greek and Egyptian Mythologies*. Chicago: University of Chicago Press, 1992.

Brewer, Douglas J., and Emily Teeter. *Egypt and the Egyptians*. New York: Cambridge University Press, 1999.

Budge, E. A. Wallis. *The Gods of the Egyptians*. 2 vols. New York: Dover Publications, 1969.

Casson, Lionel. *Daily Life in Ancient Egypt*. New York: American Heritage, 1975.

Cerny, Jaroslav. *Ancient Egyptian Religion*. Westport, Conn.: Greenwood Press, 1979.

Faulkner, R. O. *The Ancient Egyptian Book of the Dead*. Rev. and ed., Carol Andrews. New York: Macmillan, 1985.

———. *The Ancient Egyptian Coffin Texts*. 3 vols. Warminster, England: Aris and Phillips, 1973–1978.

———. *The Ancient Egyptian Pyramid Texts*. Oxford, England: Clarendon Press, 1969.

Goodrich, Norma L. *Ancient Myths*. New York: New American Library, 1960.

Griffiths, John G. *The Conflict of Horus and Seth*. Liverpool, England: Liverpool University Press, 1960.

Grimal, Nicolas. *A History of Egypt*. Cambridge, Mass.: Blackwell, 1992.

Harris, Geraldine. *Gods and Pharaohs from Egyptian Mythology*. New York: Peter Bedrick Books, 1981.

Hart, George. *Egyptian Myths*. Austin: University of Texas Press, 1990.

Herodotus, *Histories*. Trans., Aubrey de Sélincourt. New York: Penguin Books, 1972.

Hornung, Erik. *Conceptions of God in Ancient Egypt, The One and the Many*. Trans., John Baines. Ithaca, N.Y.: Cornell University Press, 1982.

Ions, Veronica. *Egyptian Mythology*. New York: Peter Bedrick Books, 1982.

James, T. G. H. *Ancient Egypt, The Land and Its Legacy*. Austin: University of Texas Press, 1988.

Lichtheim, Miriam. *Ancient Egyptian Literature*. 3 vols. Berkeley: University of California Press, 1973–1980.

Mackenzie, Donald. *Egyptian Myths and Legends*. New York: Gramercy Books, 1994.

Meeks, Dimitri and Christine Favard-Meeks, *Daily Life of the Egyptian Gods*. Trans., G. M. Goshgarian. Ithaca, N.Y.: Cornell University Press, 1993.

Millard, Anne. *Mysteries of the Pyramids*. Brookfield, Conn.: Millbrook Press, 1995.

Nardo, Don. *Cleopatra*. San Diego, Calif.: Lucent Books, 1994.

Patrick, Richard. *All Color Book of Egyptian Mythology*. London: Octopus Books, 1972.

Plutarch. *Isis and Osiris, in Moralia*. 14 vols. Trans., F. C. Babbitt. Cambridge, Mass.: Harvard University Press, 1936.

Redford, Donald B. *Akhenaten: The Heretic King*. Princeton, N. J.: Princeton University Press, 1984.

Reeves, Nicholas. *Into the Mummy's Tomb*. New York: Scholastic/Madison Press, 1992.

Shafer, Byron E., ed. *Religion in Ancient Egypt: Gods, Myths, and Personal Practice*. Ithaca, N.Y.: Cornell University Press, 1991.

Shaw, Ian, and Paul Nicholson. *The Dictionary of Ancient Egypt*. New York: Harry N. Abrams, 1995.

Spence, Lewis. *Ancient Egyptian Myths and Legends*. New York: Dover Publications, 1990.

# Index